LOW-COST SANITATION

A survey of practical experience

John Pickford

PUBLISHING

Published by ITDG Publishing
103–105 Southampton Row, London WC1B 4HL, UK
www.itdgpublishing.org.uk

Water, Engineering and Development Centre (WEDC), Loughborough University of Technology,

© John Pickford 1995

First Published in 1995

Reprinted 2001, 2006

ISBN 1 85339 233 2

A catalogue record for this book is available from the British Library.

ITDG Publishing is the publishing arm of the Intermediate technology Development Group. Our mission is to build the skills and capacity of people in developing countries through the dissemination of information in all forms, enabling them to improve the quality of their lives and that of future generations.

Some of the illustrations were drawn by the author using *Microsoft drawing*. The illustrations on the cover and some others were drawn by Rod Shaw.

Printed and bound in England by Antony Rowe Ltd, Chippenham, Wiltshire

CONTENTS

PART C
GETTING APPROPRIATE
SANITATION

Dedicated to the two billion or so people who have neither low-cost sanitation nor any other place to relieve themselves in a healthy, convenient and private way.

PART A

THE IMPORTANCE OF SANITATION

Chapter 1: SANITATION IN PERSPECTIVE

a. Why another book?

THERE ARE ALREADY many books about sanitation. Some deal primarily with technology, describing different methods of sanitation and how to design and construct them. Others are more concerned with 'software' - such things as finance, the role of agencies, local committees and women, and sharing responsibility for construction.

Many existing books are full of the authors' views about *what ought to be done* without explaining how effective the advice has been in the field. .

As far as possible this book gives evidence for and against particular methods by recounting practical experience in many countries. I have tried to tell where systems worked, how well they worked, where they were not successful, and why. It is a book about real-world sanitation. I hope the accounts of sanitation experience in varied conditions will help readers to decide what is appropriate for their own situation, whether they are

- decision-makers, advisers and planners concerned with global, regional, national and local programmes;
- professionals implementing projects and programmes for government departments, international agencies, donors and non government organizations;
- householders and communities setting out on the planning, promotion, construction, operation and maintenance of sanitation facilities;
- students and their teachers wanting a concise review of important features of appropriate sanitation based on wide experience; or
- researchers, who need to know what has already been done.

Sources of experience

*   Much of the 'practical experience' described in this book has been obtained while visiting or working in more than thirty developing countries, mostly in Africa and Asia. I have seen - and sometimes smelled - most of the different types of present-day sanitation described.

*   Information also comes from other publications, marked in the text by ®. Readers will find details in the Bibliography (Annex IV).

*   Another useful source of local experience has been some of the thousands of engineers and other professionals who have attended WEDC courses or WEDC Conferences.

You will find some accounts of what was done by low income people long ago and many descriptions of present practice world-wide — places mentioned are listed in Annex III. Generally details of construction are only described briefly, as these are covered in *A guide to the*

Franceys, Pickford & Reed, 1992

development of on-site sanitation® and other publications.

b. What is sanitation?

An account of the glory of ancient Greece claims that 'there is no truer sign of civilization and culture than good

Stobart, 1935

sanitation'.®

The word *sanitation* really refers to all conditions that affect health. In 1950 an expert committee of the World Health Organization defined 'environmental sanitation' as including such things as food handling and atmospheric pollution.

Now *environmental sanitation* sometimes includes:

* Strictly *excreta* are plural, but most people talk as if it were an English word instead of Latin; so excreta is used in this book as a singular word

*   *excreta** or *excrement* (faeces and urine);
*   *sullage* (dirty water that has been used for washing ourselves, our clothes, pots, pans, etc);
*   *drainage* (removing natural water that falls as rain or snow);
*   and *solid waste* (also called 'garbage' or 'refuse');

This book is only concerned with excreta and its treatment and disposal. This was the sense in which the word 'sanitation' was used when the 1980s were designated as the International Drinking Water Supply and Sanitation Decade, 1981-1990 (IDWSSD).

c. Sanitation coverage

When national ministries of health or international organizations refer to sanitation coverage, they usually mean the number of people or the number of households or the percentage of the total population or the percentage of all households who have places set aside for excreta disposal. Sometimes coverage counts all methods, whether they are good or bad. Other statistics for sanitation only include toilets that are judged to be satisfactory.

WHO/CWS, 1992

Annex I gives sanitation coverage for some low-income countries. According to WHO,® sanitation coverage in all developing countries increased from 46 per cent to 54 per cent during the IDWSSD. However, in 1990 there were still about 1364 million rural people and 377 urban people without what governments and international bodies count as 'adequate' sanitation.

Allowing for the expected increase in the world's population, over nine billion people would have to be provided with sanitation in the 1990s for every person to be covered by the end of the century. Full sanitation coverage is part of WHO's campaign for *Health for all by 2000.*®

However, full coverage by 2000 is an unrealistic target, so was modified to 'encouragement of hygiene awareness' for all and total latrine coverage for high risk areas.® These high risk areas are where

World Health, 1988

WHO/SEARO, 1993

- surface water is used for drinking;
- high population densities are combined with poor excreta disposal facilities; and
- there is a high incidence of excreta-related diseases.

Some local coverage data

In 1990 only 3 per cent of India's rural population was covered by sanitation, although in the Indian state of Manipur the coverage was 87 per cent.® In 1991 in neighbouring Myanmar 50 per cent of rural people had latrines, and in Yangon, the capital, nearly 99 per cent of households had them.®

GOI, 1990

CSO, 1989

Some areas and cultures have high coverage. In villages of the Nile delta over 90 per cent of houses have some sort of latrine provided by the householders themselves.® In 1978, before the start of the Decade, a survey of three villages in eastern Nigeria found that 89 per

El-Katsha et al, 1989

Egbuniwe, 1980

Harris et al, 1981

Luong *et al*, 1993

cent used pit latrines® and almost all households in Dar es Salaam had some form of sanitation.® Coverage remained high in Tanzania. In 1993 it was reported that 85 per cent of rural households and 90 per cent of urban households had latrines near their homes and used them.®

Unreliability of statistics

In Myanmar I was told that the statistics for infant mortality were low in parts of the country where timber is scarce. The quantity of wood permitted for a coffin depended on the height of the deceased. So even the smallest dead child was claimed to be six feet tall.

IRC Newsletter, 1992

Aziz et al, 1990

In Bangladesh the use of sanitary latrines was reported to have increased from four per cent to 25 per cent between 1985 and 1992.® However, another report claimed that 45 per cent of the people used latrines in 1990.® The difference between 25 per cent and 45 per cent gives an indication of the unreliability of some coverage statistics. Other examples are the figures for rural water supply coverage for 1990 in Nigeria (22 per cent by WHOand 55 per cent by UNICEF)® and for rural sanitation in India (3 per cent by WHO in 1990 and 11 per cent by the National Sample Survey in 1988-89.®

UNICEF, 1992

Huda, 1993

Sanitation in cities

It is sometimes assumed that major cities are fully sewered. Although they may be unreliable, statistics for developing countries give a very different picture. For example, in the late 1980s only two per cent of Bangkok's population was connected to sewers; Khartoum's municipal sewerage covered five per cent of the urban area. Jakarta and Kinshasa had no sewerage at all.®

Hardoy et al, 1990

d. What is appropriate sanitation?

It is that which meets the needs of people in the best possible way in relation to the resources available and other aspects of the local situation.

- **People's needs** are primarily privacy, convenience and health.
- **Resources** include availability of space, skills and above all finance. An agency that effectively facilitates the provision of latrines may be another resource.

- The **local situation** is concerned with climate, the soil, surface and underground water, traditions, religion, culture, hygiene awareness, the proximity of other people, leadership patterns and the institutions serving the people.

Improving health

Good sanitation is often linked with safe drinking water, as both reduce disease and particularly contribute to the health and well-being of children. So in the next chapter we look at some of the diseases associated with excreta, and throughout the book you will find references to ways in which disease-spreading pathogens are controlled by good sanitation.

Privacy and convenience

Privacy is very important, particularly for women, and this can even go to the extent of making sure that nobody can observe an approach to the place that must not even be mentioned!

In some places women without latrines have to defecate before dawn or after sunset. From an early age women in rural Bangladesh are trained to control themselves during daylight hours.® A story that is often repeated concerns a young woman who became an important beautician in Bombay. She still lived with her family in a slum with no latrine and told a woman's magazine 'every morning I control the urge with a great effort and rush to the toilet once I reach the beauty parlour'. ®

Agarwal, 1985

Agarwal & Anand, 1986

Because of the *purdah* system, some Muslim women can only defecate on rooftops.® In Yemen 'a corner of the roof next to a wall offers sufficient privacy for the act'.®

Moser, 1991
Al-Eshawi, 1992

Forty years ago it was reported that in villages around Cairo quite a large proportion of the people used the 'animal room' in the house.® This practice still applied in the 1980s when I was entertained by a villager near Cairo and his male friends. The householder proudly showed me his latrine. Watching and excluded from the conversation were my lady interpreter and the householder's wife. As we walked away the interpreter told me that the wife was not allowed to use the latrine. 'What does she do?' I asked. 'Oh, she has to use the cowshed'.

Weir et al, 1952

An example of the importance of privacy comes from part of Zambia where men and boys wishing to relieve themselves go out on the lake and do the necessary over the end of the canoe. Then to conceal the reason for going out they spear a fish. They are careful that their catch is not eaten by local people, but is dried and sold.®

Mwayanguba, 1991
Naipal, 1981

A Malaysian student told V S Naipal® 'You should choose, if you don't have a proper toilet, a secluded place where nobody can see you . . . and not any place where the faeces will give offence to the public: it is a holy teaching and it is applicable in our life'. Islamic law decrees that urination should be beyond the public scrutiny and should not be done . . while conversing with anyone else.®

Reynolds, 1943

In addition to giving privacy, good sanitation provides convenience. The value of this can be appreciated if you have been suffering with diarrhoea and were unable to find a nearby place to relieve yourself. The location of latrines is discussed in Chapter 3.

Availability of resources

The reason for concentrating on *low cost* sanitation requires little defence if the economic situation in developing countries is considered, for example by looking at the statistics for the gross national product (GNP) in Annex I. When deciding how to spend what little money they have, the overwhelming majority of people in these countries have many more urgent demands than expensive sanitation. With the limited resources available from internal and international sources, the lowest reasonable cost is appropriate if sanitation coverage is to be increased. Unfortunately, even low cost sanitation is too expensive for the most economically weak communities. The World Health Organization reported in 1987 that in least developed countries the median capital cost for on-site urban sanitation was twice as much as standpost water supply.

Criteria for satisfactory sanitation

LIST
1 First question   ?
2 Second question   ?
3 Third question   ?
4 Fourth question   ?
5 Fifth question   ?
6 Sixth question   ?
7 Seventh question ?
8 Eigth question   ?

Various lists have been produced to check whether existing sanitation in a community is good enough. A start may be made by looking around and asking the local people for answers to questions like the following:
- are faeces lying around where people walk or children

play?

- are water sources polluted directly or indirectly by faeces?
- where do people defecate?

If people have latrines:

- are there any problems, such as bad smell or difficulties with cleaning. repair or emptying?
- are there a lot of flies and/or mosquitoes in and around the latrines?

Several authors have listed requirements for good sanitation. These criteria for rural areas and small communities® are often quoted.

Wagner & Lanoix, 1958

Wagner and Lanoix criteria for satisfactory excreta disposal

- No surface soil contamination
- no contamination of springs or wells
- no contamination of surface water
- no access to flies or animals
- minimum handling of fresh excreta
- freedom from smells and unsightly conditions
- simple and inexpensive in construction and operation

However, it has been noted that 'to insist that any system to be adopted should fulfil all seven requirements is a counsel of perfection in-so-far as African conditions are concerned'.®

Marais® made another list when designing sanitation for low-cost housing, but it is even more difficult to satisfy all his criteria, which are as follows.

Peel, 1967
Vincent et al, 1961

Marais' criteria for satisfactory sanitation

- **should be cheap**
- **should not be communal**
- **uses little or no water**
- **operates despite misuse**
- **requires little supervision**
- **does not use soakaways**
- **disposes of all wastewater**
- **treats wastewater with little danger to users**
- **uses no mechanical equipment**

Other suggested criteria are that sanitation should be culturally acceptable to the beneficiaries, should be

Reed, 1994

Mara & Cairncross, 1989

Hardoy et al, 1992

Chaudhuri, 1965

'environmentally friendly' and should be affordable and sustainable. More specific is the government of China's criteria that latrines should be free from flies, odour and maggots.®

The environment

The environment benefits from *reuse* of wastewater and excreta.® This fits in with the current environmental concern about continually growing populations, erosion of top soil andallied problems. Pollution of water is reduced and better use of water resources is possible. Excreta is a valuable land-conditioner and fertilizer, and excreta-derived humus is better for the soil than artificial fertilizer. Energy is saved and pollution from fertilizer manufacture is eliminated. Desertification can be controlled and public open spaces improved by irrigation with treated wastewater. There are health hazards in using raw excreta, but appropriate methods of disposal can secure both health and environmental benefits.

Disposal of human waste is a major environmental concern everywhere. Where there is sewerage, the volume of wastewater discharged to streams, rivers and the sea continually increases. Pollution is often made worse by the discharge of effluents from factories. Sewerage in many developing countries is affected by lack of control, as large numbers of small workshops may discharge waste oil and other harmful substances to the sewers.

The majority of people in developing countries do not have sewers, but serious environment deterioration may be due to uncontrolled dumping of raw excreta and sludge emptied from pits, vaults and septic tanks.

Interest in the environment tends to be greatest in industrial countries, with most concern about 'greenhouse effects' and chemical agents in the air. So biological pathogens in water, food, air and water are often neglected, although they are critical environmental issues for low income countries.®

Another aspect of concern is the 'visual environment'. An eminent Indian referred to 'the sight of ubiquitous human excreta everywhere, even in a big city'.® However, objection to seeing exposed excreta is largely a cultural matter, and visible human faeces may not worry some people at all.

One environmental issue that receives a lot of attention is the pollution of groundwater. This is discussed in Chapter 7. Groundwater pollution is often cited to justify sewerage and condemn on-site methods of sanitation, particularly where nearby wells or boreholes provide drinking water. However, sewerage and sewage treatment are very expensive. It is generally less costly to pipe water to a community from a distant unpolluted source than to transport the waste away in sewers or tankers.®

Cairncross, 1992

People and communities

For low income people water supply is generally a public affair, with collection from wells or standposts. Good sanitation is often private, with a latrine for every household as the objective.

Increasing population adds to the problems of providing adequate sanitation. In many developing countries the population as a whole is doubling every ten or twenty years. With more people there is more excreta and less space for dealing with it. Overall population growth is accompanied by rapid urbanization. So the proportion of people living in towns and cities is continually increasing, creating still more sanitation problems.

Population growth in some places has caused a shortage of water available for domestic use. Even where the total quantity of water remains the same the amount available *per person* decreases as more people use it. But often the quantity does not remain the same. Competing demands by agriculture and industry reduce the quantity that people can have for domestic purposes — for drinking and cooking, for hygiene and for sanitation.

Management of sanitation

Because sanitation is primarily a private or household activity, the involvement of communities and agencies may be a matter of *enabling* individual householders to improve their sanitation. Managing latrine provision then requires promotion or encouragement. Marketing techniques may be appropriate, offering the householders a choice of systems which may be available for a range of costs. This is 'social marketing', which is different from commercial marketing as the marketer is concerned with correct use and sustainability, rather than simply selling a product.®

Simpson-Hebert, 1993

Goyder 1978

The agencies which accept responsibility for sanitation and the systems they employ are very varied.® Chapter 9 discusses some of the issues involved. In many countries several ministries deal with sanitation, with the perhaps inevitable result that each blames others for shortcomings. State companies have been formed in some Latin American countries, and elsewhere new institutions have been set up. Some separate bodies formed to implement projects funded by external grants or loans have seen their role entirely as one of provision of physical facilities by construction. When the work was completed the staff was dispersed and the facilities were passed to another body without the resources (in finance and staff) to cope.

Fortunately this attitude is now less common. There is generally more understanding of the need for sustainability, for preparation for long-term operation and maintenance, and for the involvement of communities. Engineers no longer confine their activities to engineering, but speak with understanding about such matters as hygiene promotion and the role of women in their schemes. Promotion of hygiene is increasingly seen as a crucial first step in sanitation improvement which should often come before any thought of latrine construction, At the same time there is growing appreciation of ways in which the private sector can help in the public service of providing and maintaining good sanitation.

Partly because they are 'nearer the people', voluntary agencies — Non Governmental Organizations (NGOs) — are increasingly involved in low cost sanitation. Many do excellent work, of which examples are described later. Others are sometimes accused of 'amateurism'. This is good in the sense that amateurs act because they love their work or love the people they serve. Amateurism is criticized when amateurs do not fully understand what they are doing and 'reinvent the wheel', trying out ideas that have been tried many times before, with or without success.

It is hoped that the experience recounted in this book will help volunteers and all involved in low cost sanitation projects to appreciate what others have done, and so to achieve greater success in enabling low income people to have appropriate, good and sustainable sanitation.

Chapter 2: SANITATION AND HEALTH

a. Disease and death in developing countries

THE MAIN REASONS for providing appropriate sanitation are privacy, convenience and health. Usually governments, international agencies and donors think that reduction of disease is most important, while the people themselves may like the convenience and privacy of household latrines, and sometimes want a clean environment or the prestige and status of having a latrine.

These figures from Annex I indicate how unhealthy many low-income countries are.

Child mortality (per thousand live births)			
Bangladesh	133	Bhutan	205
Ethiopia	212	The Gambia	234
India	126	Malawi	228
Mozambique	292	Nigeria	188
Pakistan	134	Sierra Leone	253
Sudan	173	Tanzania	178
Uganda	190	Zambia	200
UK	*9*	*USA*	*11*

A WHO report® stated that 'the role of unsatisfactory sanitation must be stressed as a major cause of ill health'. In the early 1980s the famous Brandt Report® referred to the millions of children who die due to water and excreta related diseases. 'All these deaths cannot be eliminated just by providing safe water and sanitation, *but* there can be no lasting improvement of public health without them'.

The improvement of health and increased life expectancy in 19th century Europe and North America has often been attributed to good water supplies and sanitation. Florence Nightingale associated drains with God® and Prince Albert was so stirred by the consequences of bad sanitation that he said he would like to be a plumber if he were not a prince.® Writing about the army in India Rudyard Kipling claimed that 'the most important medical office ought to be the provost-marshal of latrines'.

WHO, 1982

Brandt, 1980

Strachey, 1979

Lambton, 1978
Kipling, 1937

Sanitation alone is not enough. Nor is a good water supply. A third component is necessary to improve health and to decrease disease. This is *health education* or *hygiene promotion*, which is discussed in Chapter 8. In relation to sanitation the most important matters requiring hygiene education inputs are cleanliness of latrines and washing hands with soap or ash after defecation or after dealing with a child's faeces. Hand-washing after defecation is the most essential requirement to maximize health benefits.® In many cultures there are strict rules about anal cleaning. The left hand is commonly used and becomes unclean until practically or ritually cleaned.

WHO, 1992

Hygiene promotion campaigns aim to create awareness of good sanitation practices and encourage the construction and use of latrines, in addition to helping people to understand the importance of good personal hygiene.

b. Transmission of disease

WHO, 1982

Proper use of good sanitation can control diseases that are passed on in faeces or urine. An adult who has enough to eat excretes something like a million million microorganisms every day. Microorganisms are living creatures such as bacteria that are too small to be seen with the naked eye, but can be observed through a microscope. Most of those excreted are harmless. In fact they are beneficial as they help faeces and urine to break down naturally in the environment.

However, if people have diseases like those listed below® their excrement (particularly faeces) is likely to contain 'pathogens' (microorganisms or larger organisms) that pass on the diseases to other people.

Disease	People infected	Deaths per year
Cholera	More than 300 000	More than 3000
Diarrhoeal diseases	700 million or more infected each year	More than five million
Roundworm	800 - 1000 million	20 000
Bilharzia	200 million	over 200 000
Filariasis	90 million	---

These pathogens are generally swallowed with food or drink, although some enter the human body through the skin. You may have seen a diagram like this on the right, showing what are known as the faecal-oral transmission routes — the ways by which pathogens in faeces go to someone else through the mouth. These routes include water, hands, flies and other insects, soil and plants. The routes are obstructed by sanitation in various ways.

Waterborne diseases

People sometimes associate water with the transmission of diseases like dysentery, cholera, typhus and other forms of diarrhoea. So they are often called 'waterborne' or 'water carried'. Pathogens may get into streams when people excrete into or near the water, and groundwater may be polluted by pathogens even when latrines are provided. Sewerage results in pollution of streams and lakes unless the sewage is fully treated in waste stabilization ponds. Water in leaking water pipes may be contaminated by polluted water outside the pipes, especially if the supply is intermittent or pressure is low.

Treating water alone does not always ensure improved health, as shown by the mortality rates in some Indian cities during the five years before and after installing water filtration plants in the nineteenth century.®

Klein, 1973

Mortality per 1000	Before	After
Agra	32.1	35.5
Allahabad	25.8	28.7
Benares	40.0	48.8
Kanpur	41.1	47.8

Not all waterborne diseases start their transmission route with excreta. For example, guinea worm larvae are discharged through a blister that bursts when it gets wet. Some diseases are 'water-related' rather than waterborne. Malaria's connection with water is that mosquitoes live or breed in water. The spread of other diseases, such as yaws and impetigo, may be caused by people not washing themselves or their clothes properly, often because of a shortage of water. So guinea-worm, malaria and impetigo are not directly related to sanitation.

Some diseases need what are known as 'intermediate hosts' in the transmission route. Bilharzia (or

schistosomiasis) is an example. Excreta from an infected person contains eggs that hatch to release larvae in water. The larvae may penetrate water snails which later discharge other free-swimming larvae. These may bore through the skin of someone else walking or standing in the water and so infect them.

Other transmission routes

Often the diarrhoeal diseases are passed on by hands or flies. Flies are a very serious threat to health, especially in warm climates where their breeding cycle is short. They may be the main transmission route for diarrhoea.

The larvae of helminths like roundworms and hookworms may be carried to someone else when infected faeces get on the ground. This is a particular problem when children defecate onto the ground where other children crawl. Roundworm eggs remain viable (able to infect other people) for a very long time. They are therefore a serious health hazard where human excreta gets onto growing food crops, which is likely when people defecate in fields or when excreta is used as a fertilizer.

Beef and pork parasites may be transmitted when animals eat grass contaminated by human excreta. Thorough cooking avoids this danger.

Personal hygiene, which depends on sufficient water and good housing rather than sanitation, is important in preventing the transmission of some diseases, especially those, like polio and hepatitis A, where the pathogens are viruses. In a study in Lesotho® it was found that the *quantity* of water used was important in controlling the parasite which was a leading cause of acute diarrhoea. Skin and eye diseases may also be reduced or eliminated when adequate quantities of water are available.

Esray, Collett et al, 1989

Problems with wastewater

Unless adequate measures are taken, the provision or improvement of a water supply can even contribute to increasing disease in communities because more wastewater is produced.® Pools of sullage in lanes or open drains may provide breeding sites for Culex mosquitoes, some species of which pass on Bancroftian filariasis and Rift Valley fever. These mosquitoes are also referred to as culicines. Their eggs, larvae and adults look different from

WHO, 1982

Anopheles mosquitoes that transmit malaria. The adult Culex mosquito looks like this when resting.

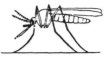

People infected with filariasis may develop painful swellings and eventually the disfiguring and painful condition known as elephantiasis. Rapid urbanization in coastal East Africa in the absence of adequate wastewater disposal led to unprecedented increases in populations of this troublesome mosquito and so Bancroftian filariasis became highly endemic.®

Kilama & Minjas, 1985

Many years of exposure to intense night-time mosquito biting are needed for filariasis to develop.® Such exposure is not uncommon. Before a campaign to control mosquitoes in Zanzibar it was estimated that each person in one town there received about twenty-five thousand bites a year. Half the population was infected with filariasis.®

WHO, 1991

Maxwell & Curtis, 1991

Survival of pathogens

Pathogens are excreted in very large numbers by infected people, and they remain in the environment for a long time, as shown in the following table for temperatures of 20°C to 30°C.® **U** gives the number of days beyond which it is most unlikely that the pathogens remain active and **M** gives the usual maximum number of days. A few roundworm eggs are able to transmit infection after a year.

Shuval et al, 1986

Pathogen	excreted load organisms per gram	SURVIVAL TIME IN DAYS							
		in faeces, sludge		in water and sewage		in soil		on crops	
		U	M	U	M	U	M	U	M
Viruses									
Enteroviruses	10^7	100	20	120	50	100	20	60	15
Bacteria									
Faecal coliforms	10^8	90	50	60	30	70	20	30	15
Salmonella spp	10^8	60	30	60	30	70	20	30	15
Shigella spp	10^7	30	10	30	10			10	5
Vibrio cholerae	10^7	30	5	30	10	20	10	5	2
Protozoa									
Entamoeba histolytica cysts	10^5	30	15	30	15	20	10	10	5
Helminths									
Roundworm eggs	10^4	many months		many months		many months		many months	

Use of treated wastewater

The reduction of pathogens in water such as in streams, rivers or canals depends on time and temperature, not on the distance travelled. So the danger of disease transmission from fast flowing water extends much further downstream than with a slow running canal or river.

Mara & Cairncross, 1989

In 1985 a meeting of experts held at Engelburg in Switzerland appraised health risks and recommended guidelines for the use of treated wastewater less stringent than those hitherto in use.® The mean number of viable roundworm, hookworm and whipworm eggs should be less than one per litre. For unrestricted irrigation on edible crops, sports fields and public parks the number of faecal coliforms should not exceed one thousand per 100ml. Irrigation of fruit trees should stop two weeks before fruit is picked and no fruit should be picked off the ground. Irrigation of pasture with treated wastewater should stop two weeks before animals are allowed to graze there.

c. **Diarrhoea and worms**

A global review by the World Health Organization commented that 'all developing countries list diarrhoea as one of the most serious problems affecting the health of the child population and one of the main reasons for contact with the health system'.®

WHO, 1987

Diseases causing diarrhoea include cholera, gastro-interitis and dysentery. They are all killer diseases. Mortality rates have been reduced by oral rehydration therapy (ORT). Even so, diarrhoea still causes the death of three million children each year.®

UNICEF, 1992

ORT consists of giving the patient water to which measured quantities of salt and sugar are added. Special ORT spoons can be used to measure the salt and sugar. In some places mothers make measuring spoons from two bottle-tops of different sizes. Although ORT prevents death from dehydration, it has little impact on the frequency or intensity of illness associated with diarrhoea.®

Feachem, 1986

Habicht *et al*, 1988

An interesting study involved over five thousand infants in peninsular Malaysia.® In all households the infant mortality rate was higher for bottle-fed children than for those who were breast-fed. Breast-feeding had greatest influence on reducing mortality for communities where there were no latrines. In these communities five times as many bottle-fed children died before their first birthday as those who were breast fed.

Proper use of latrines by everyone in a community may reduce diarrhoea. A sociological study of four similar low-income communities in Sri Lanka found that one of these communities had by far the highest incidence of diarrhoea. It was also the only community where a substantial number of people defecated in the open, on beaches and canal banks. Virtually everyone in the other three communities, each with less diarrhoea, used latrines.®

Silva & Athukorala, 1991

In most developing countries the disease problems of children are particularly severe – with malnutrition interacting with gastro-enteritis, intestinal worms, and other communicable diseases.®

Morrow, 1983

Roundworms (*ascariasis*) and similar parasites steal the food that should be used by children for energy and growth. Often the poorest children, who have least food to share with worms, have the largest number of them. Worm infection is very common. In Myanmar and other countries I have been told that intestinal worms are accepted as 'normal', with a belief in the mutually beneficial symbiosis of worms and children. 'In Africa part of the labours of sick farmers goes into the cultivation of food for the worms that make them sick'.®

Peel, 1976

It has been estimated that about a billion people (mainly children) carry a load of roundworms. Nearly as many have hookworms and more than half a billion have whipworms.®

Crompton, 1991

It is not surprising that so many people have worms. A roundworm produces 200 000 eggs per day. Hookworms can live up to seven years.® They cause the death of about 20 000 people a year,® and again most of these are children. Hookworm disease gives rise to anaemia and general debility, and in children is a cause of mental and physical retardation.®

Obeng, 1991
Esray, Potash et al, 1990

WHO, 1982

Interestingly, a study in Dakar in Senegal, West Africa, found that a third of peri-urban people had roundworms, but less than one in a hundred of the nearby rural population had them. Dirty latrines where the floors are fouled with faeces may present a serious danger of transmission of worm diseases. This hazard may be worse than where people practice open defecation.®

Cairncross, 1988

d. Evidence of health benefits

Sceptical bureaucrats and funding agencies sometimes want evidence that latrines are cost-effective. Unfortunately, health impacts of good sanitation are difficult to quantify.

Moreover, there is little correlation between health improvements and the provision of sanitation unless there is *adequate* provision — a threshold must be reached.® It is illustrated in this graph indicating health benefits against the proportion of households with latrines. Good sanitation is a 'public good' because it benefits other people — or to put it the other way round, the health of people who have good sanitation may suffer if some of their neighbours practice indiscriminate defecation. Full sanitation coverage is necessary for full health benefit. If only five or ten per cent of people in a neighbourhood defecate in the open, the health of the whole community may suffer.

Kawata, 1978

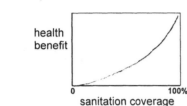

Cost of disease

It is difficult to make a cost-benefit analysis showing that sanitation improvements are justified on economic grounds. However, the Peru cholera epidemic in the early 1990s provided information about the cost of *not* providing good sanitation and water supply. In the first ten weeks of the epidemic losses in agricultural exports and revenues from tourism were more than three times the total amount Peru invested in sanitation and water supply in the whole of the 1980s.®

World Bank, 1992

The reduction of diseases when good sanitation is provided and properly used has economic benefits. The diseases that are common in situations with bad sanitation may result in reduced productivity.® In addition, economic losses may result from:

Simpson-Hebert, 1993

- time spent looking after sick children;
- reduced education due to absence from school and inability of sick children to learn properly;
- wasted family expenditure on medicine and fees for medical attention; and
- wasted public expenditure in hospitals and health clinics.

By 1980 there was a general decline in the use of health criteria in project design because agencies could not show conclusively that sanitation investments had direct health outcomes.® Even so, a few statistical indicators of the health benefits of sanitation can be quoted.

Warner & Laugeri, 1991

Reduced mortality and illness

Among about 2500 infants in Bangladesh® mortality was 3.12 times higher in households not using latrines than in those who did use them. In a study in Madras® the weight and height of children was compared for different age groups. Use of latrines by the whole family was most beneficial for 18-month to 36-month age children.

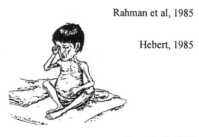

Rahman et al, 1985

Hebert, 1985

The health impact of water supply and sanitation was studied over a four year period in the dry zone of Upper Myanmar.® It was found that there was little change in health from provision of improved water alone, that provision of latrines had a greater impact than provision of good water, and that the greatest health improvement was when both sanitation and water were improved. In nine villages diarrhoea affected 3.05 per cent of those with latrines compared with 7.62 per cent of those with no latrines. So latrines reduced diarrhoea by 60 per cent.®

Rosenhall, 1990

Myint & Aye, 1988

Reduced incidence of worm diseases

This table shows the incidence of intestinal parasites amongst 650 pre-school children in four villages in Ghana in the 1980s.®

Annan, 1985

Rate of worm infection

	indiscriminate defecation	pit latrine	bucket latrine
roundworm	76%	30%	40%
hookworm	70%	4%	10%

The children in one village, Oshiyie, harboured on average twice as many infections as the children in the other villages. The only explanation of the difference was that in Oshiyie indiscriminate defecation around the houses and in the fields was normal despite the presence of communal latrines.®Pre-school children would be expected to defecate near their homes rather than in latrines, but the habits of the older people affected the health of all.

Annan et al, 1986

In twelve hundred houses in Costa Rica the incidence of roundworm disease was nearly 70 per cent for households with no latrine, about 39 per cent where pit

Moore et al, 1965

latrines were used and only 26 per cent where there were septic tanks.®

Reduced diarrhoea

Esray, Feachem et al, 1985

A literature review by the World Health Organization's Diarrhoeal Diseases Control Programme reported a median reduction in diarrhoea morbidity of 22 per cent with improved sanitation.® On the other hand, a study of diarrhoea amongst under-five children in Sri Lanka found little variation between families with or without latrines. The crucial requirement for improved health seemed to be hygiene behaviour — how mothers deal with faeces dropped by children in the compound.®

Mertens et al, 1992

Mistaken ideas and good understanding

It is commonly and wrongly believed that children's excreta is less harmful than that of adults. A survey of 7900 individuals in rural India® showed that the general understanding was that the excreta of unweaned infants is 'absolutely harmless' as it only comes from mothers' milk. In the same survey 63 per cent of people thought exposed excreta was harmful, but there was a strong belief that it is bad smells which transmit disease.

GOI, 1990

Clarke, 1984

In a study in north west Pakistan three quarters of the people were convinced of the danger of both adult and baby excreta, but half knew none of the diseases. The excreta-related disease mentioned most often was malaria, which is incorrect in any case. Cholera was known by a few but only five persons out of the 252 questioned knew that diarrhoea can be spread by excreta.® In many places there is belief that disease 'comes from God', so good hygiene practices are irrelevant.

Health benefits from sanitation come about when good toilets are available for all members of a community, when the sanitation system is properly operated and maintained, and when toilet use is accompanied by good personal hygiene. Hand-washing after defecation, and after cleaning an infant's bottom when it has defecated, is an essential part of personal hygiene. Consequently its importance is stressed in most hygiene promotion and hygiene education programmes.

Chapter 3: SANITATION ALTERNATIVES

Technology and software

A NUMBER OF different technologies may be appropriate for low and medium income householders and communities. Part B of this book examines these alternatives and how well they function. Alternative methods may also be suitable for implementing the technologies. These are the 'software' of sanitation, which are considered in Part C.

Several authors have contrasted sanitation technology with non-technological aspects. For example it has been noted that changing technology is easier than changing behaviour.® construction is easier to achieve than latrine use® and people should define their own needs and priorities.® Much time and effort is required to ensure that the technology is what people themselves want.

Elmendorf & Buckles, 1980

Burgers et al, 1988

Harpham et al, 1988

a. In the open

Where families are scattered with plenty of space around them, defecation in the fields may not be too unsatisfactory. There is nobody to intrude on privacy and all members of a family may already have the same excreta-related diseases.

A 1990 survey in rural India found that 31 per cent of people preferred outdoor defecation, mentioning benefits like fresh air and no smell. However, many respondents said it was difficult at night and others mentioned lack of privacy and a long walk required to find a suitable place.®

GOI, 1990

In an isolated area of Nigeria, a community laughed at the foolishness of glorifying excreta by building a house for it. They were angry with the authorities for trying to impose such a mad practice. However, to avoid imprisonment of their chief, the community built three latrines in 1986 to comply with a government order. As advised by the government, the latrines were roofed and had doors. The people then locked the doors and deposited the keys with the chief. Itinerant sanitary inspectors were very pleased when they visited the village, commending the people on how clean the latrines were kept.®

Ugbe, 1990

Why people like the open air

An American in charge of an Indian mobile health team, whose husband was an Indian university teacher, told a visitor 'the one half-hour in which a woman can get away from the kids and the mother-in-law is between 4.30 and 5 in the morning, when she and her friends get together in the fields, squatting and talking'.®

Hopcraft, 1968

In the Philippines during an investigation to find out why few people built latrines, one farmer said 'we have something better than the odorous thing you are offering. Our latrine is a five hectare area behind my house, where the faecal matter is automatically dried by the sunshine and does not smell. It is even good fertilizer for my plants'.® Some people object to latrines because they are unwilling to share them with others.® Open defecation is sometimes favoured because people like to see their faeces — for example to find out whether they have worms.

Feliciano & Flavier, 1967

Hubley, 1987

Even from a health point of view latrines may not always be beneficial. It is reported that in hot dry countries of North Africa defecation in open fields results in less transmission of disease that the use of cheap pit latrines.®

Agarwal, 1981

Disadvantages of open defecation

There may be a danger of spread of hookworm where people defecate in a common open place, especially if the ground is damp or marshy. This can be reduced by making ridges and furrows, as in some banana plantations. People walk on the ridges, put their feet on them when they squat and defecate into the furrows.®

Kochar, 1978

Deuteronomy

Trouble starts where people live together in groups. Moses found this in the Sinai desert with the twelve tribes of Israel. So he gave the order to go outside the camp with a stick, dig a hole and then cover the faeces with soil.® Some people now keep a spade or hoe by the door to take when they go out to defecate. Cholera returned to Mexico in the early 1990s, with six thousand cases in the first half of 1993. The Health Ministry advised 'in areas where there are no toilet facilities, people should cover their excrement with lime or earth.®

Davidson, 1993

Open defecation becomes more of a nuisance in large communities. In one year the police commissioner of Calcutta prosecuted one hundred and forty thousand people for so-called 'creating a nuisance in a public place'.®

Pathak, 1985

Wrap and carry

'Wrap and carry' or 'wrap and throw' is used in some villages and towns and even in cities like Metro Manila.® In Kibera, a city in Kenya with a population of 400 000, people defecate into plastic bags.® In Uganda where a sewerage system had broken down people bought polythene bags for wrap and carry. Many families used two bags each day, one for adults and the second one for children. After use the bags were kept until the evening when they were dumped in refuse skips.® In Chad many people use 'parcel latrines'. They defecate on a piece of plastic, wrap it to make a parcel and sometimes throw the parcel onto the roofs of neighbouring buildings, where it dries in the sun.® Other people use leaves or paper.

Ilustre, 1980

Munyakho, 1992

Muwonce, 1993

It has been suggested that wrap and carry is the most common method of disposal where there are suitable places for dumping such as the sea or swamp land close by.® Incidentally, wrap and carry has been recommended for those enjoying outdoor activities in the United States.®

Smith, 1994

Etherton, 1980

Meyer, 1989

Use of latrines

A survey in rural India found that only 2 per cent of illiterate people used latrines, but 13 per cent of those who could read used them.® In the same study 86 per cent of the 7900 individuals surveyed thought that there was advantage in having a private latrine, and only 15 per cent said they were unwilling to pay. A survey in Sri Lanka found that 94 per cent of the adults and 90 per cent of the children in 629 households surveyed used the latrines that had been provided three or more years before. ®

GOI, 1990

Danida, 1991

In the late 1930s many people in Uganda were afraid to use latrines because their fixed location would give sorcerers easy access to excreta for hostile purposes.® The authorities overcame this fear by advocating deeper pits where the excreta would be out of the sorcerers' reach.

Gillanders, 1940

Women's use of latrines

Sixty years later some tribes in Uganda believed that females who use pit latrines become infertile. So only men used the pit provided in a UNICEF project.® Other tribes do not allow pregnant women to use pit latrines; they must go to the bush.® In some villages in southern Ethiopia women were not allowed to defecate in the same place as

Ssozi, 1991

Bomukama, 1983

Davis *et al*, 1993

men. So they could not use new latrines built by the Ministry of Health.®

On the other hand, in many Muslim communities women are the main beneficiaries of latrine provision. For example, it has been reported that latrines in Egyptian villages are mainly used by the women, although some prefer to defecate on the roof. Men are more inclined to use the facilities at the mosque.® Similarly in Bangladesh, it was claimed in 1990 that women particularly favour the use of latrines because of the privacy they give.®

El-Katsha et al, 1989

Aziz et al, 1990

Convenience is a commonly-felt reason for using sanitation. In a Maharashtra village the women who were most interested in having their own household latrines were those living in the village centre. The reason was that they had to walk further to defecation areas outside the village.®

Sundaraman, 1986

Children's use of latrines

In many developing countries children are not encouraged to use latrines, sometimes because it is believed that children's faeces are 'harmless'. Children's non-use of latrines is widely reported.® Schoolchildren in Kenya mentioned the following fears when using latrines.®

Gibbs, 1984
UNCHS, 1986b

Fears associated with	Percentage of children
snakes and other animals	86
falling into the pit	56
smells, filth and insects	48
black magic	35
being left alone	14

In rural Bangladesh a survey found that nearly half the children did not use latrines, although most of the adults did,® and it has been reported that children in Yemen do not use latrines at all.® Fear of the dark inside the shelter and fear of falling into the pit are common reasons for not using latrines.®

Gibbs, 1984
Al-Eshawi, 1992

Chadha & Strauss, 1991

Men and latrines

Probably the most common reason given for not having a latrine is that householders cannot afford them, or claim they cannot.® As they usually have to pay, rural men have

Pickford, 1993

to be convinced of the value of sanitation. Their only experience of latrines may be the dirty public ones at railway stations and lorry parks, so they do not think latrines encourage cleanliness. Fit and hard-working farmers see no evidence that sanitation improves health if they compare themselves with latrine-using townspeople.® The only valid reason for latrines they see may be that latrines might provide fertilizer.

'Gender issues' are often mentioned in relation to sanitation, emphasizing the importance of the 'role of women'. So it is interesting to read that most men in a sanitation programme in the Philippines admitted they had been convinced to join by their wives or mothers.® Men in northern Pakistan said that the reason for installing latrines was to provide privacy for women rather than for health or hygiene considerations.

Sanitation usually comes well down the list of rural people's priorities, well below water, clinics and roads.® Sometimes the most successful motivation is pride or social pressure. In northern Ghana a common boast of the Gonga men is to say 'I have built a better latrine than you have'.® People in five Nepalese urban centres were asked why they had built latrines outside the government subsidized programme. Only 28 per cent of respondents gave health as the reason; 43 per cent gave prestige, comfort, privacy or a combination of these.®

An Oxfam funded latrine programme in southern Sudan was far from successful in spite of trying out several methods of low cost construction. Eventually it became clear that people were not interested in health or environmental aspects of sanitation. Low cost methods of construction did not attract them. The only effective inducement was enhanced status, which involved costs that were not always the lowest of the alternatives.® The status in having a latrine depends on what other people can see, which is the shelter.

b. Shelter and location

A provocative journal article asked 'Why should a latrine look like a house?'® Usually householders are particularly concerned with the part of the latrine that is technically known as the 'superstructure' — the part that can be seen and often looks like a little house.

Misra, 1988

Cairncross, 1992

University of Zimbabwe, 1982

Bawa, 1987

UNCHS, 1986a

Franceys, 1988

Brandberg, 1985

Privacy and protection

A pour-flush latrine or simple pit latrine operates perfectly well whether there is a shelter above it or not, although a VIP latrine must have a shelter to ensure that there is less light above the squat hole than above the vent.

A shelter over a badly-maintained latrine may be more unpleasant than the open air, where the wind carries smells away. Flies, mosquitoes and cockroaches are nuisances in shelters. A shelter makes no difference to a latrine's disease transmission, but provides other benefits that latrine owners and users generally think are important.

For UNICEF's water and sanitation programme in Bangladesh it was claimed that the home-made simple pit latrine made of bamboo and timber should be the backbone of the sanitary revolution.® Nevertheless, a few years earlier Bangladeshis were asked what they thought of latrines that were provided free. Most householders said the quality of the shelter was more important than the type of technology. Latrines were used more, especially by women, if the shelter was good and provided privacy.®

For many people the shelter is important because it enables them to relieve themselves out of sight, as discussed on page 5. Women are usually anxious not to be seen during menstruation, and some people have religious rules that require them to be unobserved while defecating or urinating. This privacy can often be adequately provided by a shelter consisting of a screen wall made, for example, with grass matting. Adequate shelters can be built with local materials such as poles and matting. In Botswana some concrete floor slabs were made with holes for upright poles that could be inserted by householders building a simple shelter.®

If a shelter is spiral in plan like the one shown here, a person squatting inside cannot be seen from outside, even if no door is fitted. Some people put a piece of string across the entrance to show that the latrine is in use. People who are defecating often cough when they hear someone approaching, announcing that the latrine is occupied Even with a door some people like to be able to see who is approaching a latrine. Lem Putt makes a special point of users being able to see who is approaching when describing 1930s privies in the mid-west of the United States in his amusing best-seller *'The Specialist'*.® A small hole was made in the door at eye level through which the path to the

Wan, 1992

Gibbs, 1984

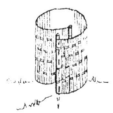

Wilson, 1983

Sale, 1930

latrine could be observed.

While a screen can provide ample privacy it provides no protection from rainfall or summer sun. A roof is especially important where there is much rain or very high temperatures. Without a roof, wind-blown debris, leaves, twigs and the like may cause malfunctioning, as happened in Srinagar. Householders had to build their own shelters for pour-flush latrines that were provided without charge. Many householders did not give their shelters roofs. ®

Sarma & Jansen, 1989

Some people display amazing ingenuity when building latrine shelters. In South Africa a grandmother collected empty milk cartons which she filled with a mixture of soil, ash and water. She used these as a kind of brick infilling with a frame of poles and twigs and then plastered the whole with mud fortified with cow-dung.®

Nene, 1991

Doors of shelters

Doors of rectangular VIP latrines should be kept closed so that the inside is dark. Doors can be kept shut by using rising butt hinges, springs or counterweights on the end of a length of string. Another simple way of making sure the door shuts is to make the frame slightly 'out of plumb' (not quite vertical). If the top of the frame leans by about 50 mm the door swings back — for an outward opening door the top of the frame should slope inwards; the frame for an inward opening door should slope outwards. Costs are sometimes saved by using a curtain or piece of sacking for privacy instead of a door.

Prestige and status

In many countries the strongest motivation for house owners to build latrines is the prestige this gives. Centuries ago the abbot of St Albans in England built a latrine 'than which none can be found more beautiful or more sumptuous'.® In Sri Lanka it was reported that 'having a toilet is associated by villagers with material and social development and progress'.® The appearance is often of great importance to the proud owner.

Wright, 1960

Hoefnagels et al, 1986

There can be competition between neighbours regarding who has the best-looking shelter. In the periurban area of a large African city I have seen white flags flying outside houses, proclaiming that there is a latrine at the back. The man with any sort of latrine has the edge on his

Anankum, 1991

Isely et al, 1986

Wright, 1960

Wegelin-Schuringa, 1991

Roy, 1990

Wagner & Lanoix, 1958

Sale, 1930

neighbour without one. Desire for prestige often results in latrines being the best-built buildings. Latrines with concrete block walls and corrugated metal roofs are often seen in villages where all the houses have mud walls and thatched roofs.

Sometimes it is not the owners' pride that leads to fine shelters. When designed by outside agencies the shelter is sometimes too good, as discussed in Chapter 9. In Togo a Canadian NGO provided Ventilated Improved Pit latrines much better than the houses. As the latrines were called 'VIPs' some people assumed they were for very important persons (also 'VIPs') and kept them for visiting dignitaries. ®

Separate latrines for men and women

In many places there is a preference for separate latrines for men and women, so in some schemes houses and their latrines have been paired. Two houses share two latrines, one used by the women of both households and the other by the men. Some societies believe that mixing of male and female faeces makes people sterile. Women's menstrual blood is particularly potent (or perhaps impotent!).®

Comfortable latrines

A latrine should be comfortable to use. Long ago at Winchester the king of England had a toilet (called a *garderobe)* built in the chimney breast for warmth.®

In an effort to reduce costs the consultant designed very small latrines in one World Bank programme in Africa with which I was involved. Because there was not enough room to move easily inside the latrines, most people did not use them.

The recommended minimum inside size for a shelter has been given as one metre by 900 mm,® although 900 mm by 750 mm is acceptable in India.® A recommended distance between a squat hole and the back wall is 150 mm. ®

However, Lem Putt suggested that latrines for use while at work should not be too comfortable.® He claimed that changing from a smooth rounded hole in the seat to one with hard edges reduced the time wasted in the latrine from forty minutes to four minutes!

c. Where to put the latrine

To reduce the possibility of water pollution, regulations and manuals often require pit latrines to be 15 metres from a well. Old regulations stipulated fifty feet. While it is useful to have a simple rule-of-thumb, in some situations there is no danger of pollution if pits are closer. The safe distance depends on the type of soil and movement of groundwater.

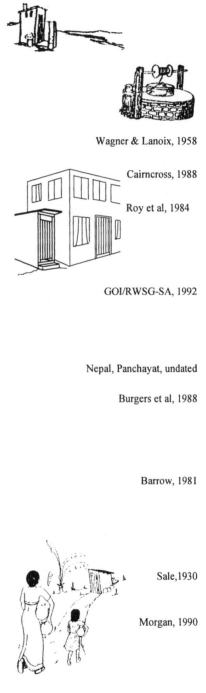

Conflicting advice is given regarding the distance of a pit from a building. Wagner and Lanoix® recommended that pits should be at least six metres from buildings. It has also been suggested® that pits should be at least three metres from the nearest wall unless there is no danger to the house foundation. Indian practice® is for a lined pit to come right up to the building wall, and even to be underneath a building, although another recommendation is that for safety pits up to 1.7 metres deep should be located 500mm from the foundation of a building. ®

Wagner & Lanoix, 1958

Cairncross, 1988

Roy et al, 1984

Those building pit latrines in Nepal were advised to make sure that full attention is given to users' preference for a suitable latrine location. 'Consciously or unconsciously, users might have cultural or religious reasons for wanting to place the latrine at a given distance and location relative to their or their neighbour's house.'®

GOI/RWSG-SA, 1992

The need to locate latrines so that users can enter without being seen has been noted in some cultures.® In East Africa many latrines were built in a quick campaign. To inspect construction easier, the public health staff sited them along the roadside. The latrines were hardly used, as the people did not like entering in full view of passers-by.®

Nepal, Panchayat, undated

Burgers et al, 1988

Lem Putt also discusses the need to allow for the embarrassment some people feel at being seen going into the latrine, and suggests that a pile of firewood should be put near the path from the house. Then a shy girl who notices she is being observed can pick up some wood and return to the house. Some girls carry several loads of wood before entering the latrine unobserved. ®

Barrow, 1981

A similar advantage is provided when a latrine is used for bathing, as in some cultures it is acceptable to be seen going to have a bath.® People in many places like to take a bucket of water to the latrine and bath after defecation. In northern Ethiopia people declined to use new latrines because they had been built where there were no trees with

Sale, 1930

Morgan, 1990

Munir, 1991

leaves suitable for anal cleaning.®

In remote mountainous villages in South Africa where everyone defecated in the open, people were asked where they would like latrines. More than three-quarters preferred 'within the boundaries of their property'. The most common reason for choosing a particular location was to

Hall & Adams, 1991

avoid the smell of faeces reaching the house.®

Location for Muslims

Reynolds, 1943

A traditional rule is that Muslims should not defecate facing Mecca or with their backs towards the holy city.® Therefore it is usually recommended that latrines should be located sideways to Mecca.

After numerous master plans for sewerage in Kumasi, Ghana, had come to nothing, it was eventually agreed to encourage pit latrines. Media interest was aroused when the first demonstration unit was completed, but the fortunate householder refused to use it. He was a Muslim and the latrine faced Mecca. There is a similar story from Bangladesh. The first two water seal latrines in a programme were built at the government's expense in the middle of a primary school playground. Religious leaders noticed that users were squatting with their backs to Mecca

Kotalova, 1984

and the latrines had to be rebuilt.®

Yacoob & Roark, 1990

Because the Koran enjoins ablution after defecation, a soakaway to absorb water from ablutions is sometimes provided outside latrines in Muslim areas.®

Congested sites

Population density in many slums and shanty towns is very high, as indicated by these examples of densities expressed as persons per hectare.

Flanagan, 1988
Dwyer, 1975
Dwyer, 1975
Lea & Courtney, 1985
Goethert et al, 1979
Hardoy *et al*, 1992

Colombo (Henemulla)	1670®
Ibadan (core area)	1500-2000®
Karachi	more than 2400®
Metro Manila	almost 2000®
Nairobi (Mathare Valley)	1600®
Shanghai	more than 1500®

In a paper dealing with *the environment of poverty*, the authors described how 'the Third World's cities are swelling as farmers and villagers hark to the siren call of a better life. But up to half the inhabitants of most of these cities wind up in slums and shanty towns' where sanitation and health care are mere dreams, while dysentery, malnutrition and cramped conditions are daily realities.®

Statistics concerning Indian overcrowding tell us that 65 per cent of families in Ahmedabad and 70 per cent of families in Calcutta live in one room.®

When it comes to authorized buildings, there is considerable variation in the minimum permitted plot size for new houses. A plot may be 50 square metres in El Salvador or 64 square metres in Botswana. In Barbados the smallest plot is 280 square metres and in Zimbabwe it is 300 square metres.®

Opponents of pit latrines often claim that they are unsuitable for small plots in urban areas. It has been argued that a 'safe' distance between pits and shallow wells requires population densities less than 150 - 200 people per hectare.®

In Jamaica there was a regulation that pit latrines should not be constructed on plots with higher density than ten houses per acre (23 houses per hectare). In Indonesia 'project areas with over 250 persons per hectare shall be classified as densely populated and shall not use on-site excreta disposal facilities'. Some writers are even more sweeping, such as the statement in a manual prepared for Habitat that the pit latrine system (except for VIPs) is 'unsuitable for use in even low density urban developments'.®

The recommendation that VIP latrines are the only type of pit latrines suitable for urban areas is interesting because another authority claims that VIPs are *only* satisfactory in windy rural settings.® These are both examples of writers asserting views of 'what ought to be done' without definite evidence.

A government review of sanitation in Nepal noted that 'in relatively high density urban communities the pour-flush twin pit latrine appears to be successful' A study of twin pit pour-flush latrines in Srinagar found plots ranging from 20 to 1800 square metres.® It was concluded that plot size had no relevance to satisfactory installation.

The smallest plot size recommended for twin pit latrines in India is 26 square metres.® With careful planning and construction double pits can be built on plots as small as twenty square metres. Alternatively, pits can be dug under lanes, the pans being within adjacent buildings.

Hardoy & Satterthwaite, 1985

UNESCAP, 1984

Struyk, 1988

Alaerts et al, 1991

Roberts, 1987

Mara, 1976

Nepal, no date

Sarma & Jansen, 1989

Ribeiro, 1985

Sinha & Ghosh, 1990

Colin, 1992

In Bihar many households failed to convert dry latrines to pour-flush although funds were available. Less than one per cent gave 'lack of space' as the reason for not taking advantage of the scheme.®

The recommendation that VIP latrines should always be on open sites is challenged by the large number that appear to be quite satisfactory when surrounded by walls or tall buildings. For example, because of the Muslim requirement that women must be secluded, Afghan refugees in Peshawar built high walls around their plots. VIPs latrines had already been built and the new walls did not interfere with the removal of smells and control of flies.®

d. Sanitation alternatives

Cultural variations and preferences

THERE ARE wide cultural variations in defecation practice. For example:

Some people . . .	but others . . .
defecate in the open	prefer a sheltered place
defecate in or near water	use a dry place
defecate in or near the house	get right away from the house
squat	sit
defecate at sunrise and sunset	relieve themselves whenever the need arises
use water for anal cleaning	use paper, leaves, sticks, stones, corncobs, etc

Apart from personal preferences, some customs are controlled by religious or social taboos such as:
- not being seen defecating or even going to a latrine;
- the direction faced when defecating;
- strict separation of men and women;
- ritual bathing before or after defecation;
- no defecation near a cemetery or near a sacred place (such as a rock or old tree); and
- faeces cannot be handled, even when decomposed.

Some customs relate to urination as well as defecation. For

example, a strict Brahmin twists his sacred thread round his ear when urinating.®

Thacker, 1993

In north-east Pakistan I was told in 1994 that there was a high incidence of kidney infections amongst women teachers and college students owing to drinking nothing during the day. The women avoided drinking because they were not permitted to urinate during working hours. or even during the whole of daylight.

In Yucatan a community traditionally used the bush for defecation. Strong preference was expressed for seats (rather than squatting slabs) and water flush WCs. This was thought to be because the community had contact with nearby tourist centres. The people also considered the colour of the floor to be important.®

Elmendorf & Buckles, 1980
Clarke, 1984

A study in villages of north-west Pakistan® asked those who have no latrines (the majority of the people) what type they would prefer. About half expressed a preference for a pour-flush latrine, and most had enough water for flushing.

Even when building a pit latrine, sitting — rather than squatting — is particularly favoured by people who think a WC is a 'better' form of sanitation. In Lesotho, for example, ventilated improved pit (VIP) latrines were provided with pedestal seats made of glass reinforced plastic (GRP).®

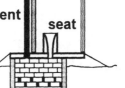

Makhatha, 1987

Women were not willing to use latrines designed by male engineers for an El Salvador project because a gap at the bottom of the door exposed their feet, offending their notions of privacy.®

Moser & Peake, 1987

All the respondents in a survey of 27 projects in Yemen complained about the smell from their existing latrines.® In Juba, Sudan, nearly half the pit latrine owners said 'smell' was their chief complaint.®

Mullick, 1987
Nichols, 1982

A thorough study of use of five types of latrine was made in a village near Chittagong, Bangladesh.® Overwhelmingly the factor which was of most importance in determining users' perception of which types were bad or good was the smell or lack of smell.

Bangladesh RWSESP, 1983

Things that many people liked about their own latrines were privacy, being close to the house, durability and absence of flies. About a third of respondents did not like their latrines because they were not suitable for children, who could not use them.

Children's latrines

At the insistence of villagers in a Sri Lanka programme, special children's latrines were built near the kitchens where mothers could train their children in their use.®

In Tanzania special children's latrines without a shelter were dug.®

An interesting variation was seen near Dodoma, the capital city. It was built as a rectangular spiral with two squat holes. A smaller one for children was placed so that the mother, also defecating, could attend to a child in front of her.® Where a latrine has a seat and a child is too short to reach it, a concrete block or stone can be put near the seat to put the feet on.®

In Ghana a survey of rural sanitation® also sought the views of children by interviewing those between the ages of seven and eleven. When conducting surveys about people's defecation practices and preferences, adult respondents are sometimes unwilling to talk about such private matters. One way of overcoming this is to discuss these matters with children, who are often less shy.

Satisfaction with latrines

In a survey in Kumasi® the percentage of householders who considered their existing sanitation as 'poor' (**P**), 'fair' (**F**) and 'good' (**G**) was as follows.

	Public latrines			Private bucket latrines			WCs			Pit latrines		
	P	**F**	**G**	**P**	**F**	**G**	**P**	**F**	**G**	**P**	**F**	**G**
Cleanliness	37	53	10	6	47	47	3	31	66	4	52	44
Privacy	54	44	2	3	71	26	1	59	40	5	84	11
Convenience	70	27	3	8	63	29	3	52	45	18	70	12
Satisfaction	71	28	1	34	55	11	8	54	38	37	57	6

Finding out what people want

It is very difficult to find out what people *really* want. Surveys can be biased by the wording of questions or even by the tone of voice of the evaluator. Household surveys often try to ensure that the sample is representative of all heads of households. In Papua New Guinea the best method

Fernando, 1982
Wegelin-Schuringa, 1991

Makwali, 1992

Mathebula, 1987
Wright et al, 1978

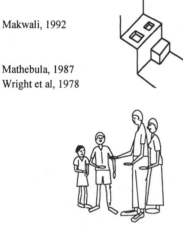

Whittington et al, 1992

to find out whether latrines are used and kept clean was found to be to ask to use the latrine. ® Presumably this cannot be done very often.

Boot & Cairncross, 1993

When people at Wanging'ombe® in Tanzania were offered a choice of latrines, a high proportion opted for compost latrines.® But many of those who chose them had no idea how they functioned. Their preference was simply because the demonstration compost latrines had permanent good shelters, while the alternative pit latrines were built of limited-life local materials.

Blakely *et al*, 1985

Cairncross, 1992

In the Kumasi 'willingness to pay' survey a basic choice was between sewerage and KVIP latrines.® No difference was found between respondents who were questioned on their own and those who answered with a group of curious neighbours around. Some respondents were given a day to think again and then more said they preferred KVIPs. The most likely reason for this change was that sewerage was a novel idea which at first seemed attractive. On reflection and discussion with neighbours, some of the disadvantages of sewerage became apparent.

Whittington et al, 1992

e. Classification of methods

Sometimes systems are divided into 'wet' and 'dry', the wet systems being those where water transports excreta. A further division can be between 'on site' and 'off site' methods. With 'on site' the main treatment of excreta is on the same plot as the house or other building.. With 'off site' methods excreta is removed from the plot.

	Wet	*Dry*
On site	Pour flush pit latrines	Other pit latrines
	Septic tanks & soakaways	Compost latrines
Off site	Sewerage	Bucket latrines
	Overhung latrines	Vault latrines

A more useful classification may be that shown in the table on the next page. All the systems listed are described in later chapters of this book.

Conventional sewerage and conventional septic tanks are high-cost systems. As people increase their standards of living their expectations usually rise. They may have moved from mud and thatch (or shelters made from bits of scrap) to a proper house with cement or better floors. A

piped water supply is expected next, then water outlets in the house. It is then a logical step to want cistern-flushed WCs, which need sewers or septic tanks.

However, cistern-flushed WCs are only suitable for people with low incomes where suitable infrastructure already exists, for example where low-income housing is in an area with existing piped water and existing sewers. For large multi-storied blocks of apartments WCs may be the only satisfactory option for household sanitation.

Other systems — low-cost sanitation — are appropriate for the majority of low-income people. The most common form of low-cost sanitation is a pit latrine, so the next Chapter is devoted to the many variations of the pit.

Classification of excreta disposal methods

	See this section for details ↓	
DECOMPOSITION	compost latrines	*5b*
	algae tanks	*5c*
DECOMPOSITION + INFILTRATION	PIT LATRINES	
	simple pits	*4a*
	pits with lids	*4c*
	VIP latrines	*4d*
	pour-flush latrines	*4e*
	twin pits	*4f*
	miscellaneous variations	*4h*
	aqua-privies + soakaways	*7c*
REMOVAL + DECOMPOSITION + INFILTRATION	SEPTIC TANKS	*7a/b*
REMOVAL	PIPE SYSTEMS	
	conventional sewerage	*6d*
	non-conventional sewerage	*6e*
	vacuum systems	*6e*
	container systems	*6a*
	vaults	*6b*
	chemical toilets	*6a*
	Overhung latrines	*6c*

PART B
APPROPRIATE SANITATION SYSTEMS

Chapter 4: PIT LATRINES

a. The pit and its size

IN ALL TYPES of pit latrine excreta falls into a hole in the ground, where faeces decompose. In the pit:

- gaseous products (mainly carbon dioxide and methane, but also small quantities of malodorous gases and vapours) are given off and escape to the atmosphere or are absorbed by the soil;
- water, urine, dissolved products of decomposition, some suspended particles and some microorganisms infiltrate the bottom and sides of the pit into the surrounding soil; and
- a solid residue accumulates in the pit, gradually coming to resemble rich soil.

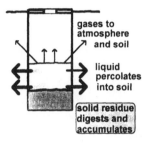

gases to atmosphere and soil

liquid percolates into soil

solid residue digests and accumulates

Types of pit latrine

There are several forms of pit latrine. The excreta may fall directly into a pit beneath the user, and the latrine is then a *direct pit*. Excreta, usually with water used for flushing and anal cleaning, may pass along a pipe or channel to an *offset pit* a few metres away. In some types the pit is *partly offset*. Part of the pit is under the shelter and part is outside, where a removeable cover allows the contents to be taken out.

The most appropriate type of pit latrine depends on the local situation, including the level of the groundwater and the traditions and culture of the users. The material used for anal cleaning after defecation is particularly important. It may be water or it may be solid material such as paper, leaves and corncobs. If solid material is used for cleaning, pits are normally under squat holes or seats so that excreta falls directly into the pits. In permeable soils pit latrines can accept small quantities of sullage, such as that which is produced when water is carried from a pond, well or

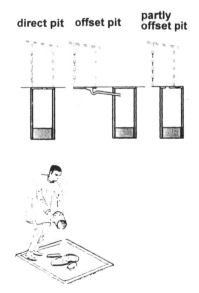

direct pit   offset pit   partly offset pit

Pickford, 1994

Franceys, 1990

standpost.

Various ways of controlling nuisance from flies and bad smells in pit latrines are described in later sections. Other variations depend on the type of soil and the depth of groundwater or hard rock. Some pits are for temporary use, others are more-or-less permanent. There may be several types of pit latrine that are appropriate, some costing more than others.® Householders may then be offered alternatives from which they can choose.®

The popularity of pit latrines

Many politicians, administrators and engineers discount pit latrines in favour of 'modern systems'. Yet even in the 1970s, before the Water Decade made appropriate technology more popular, the proportion of households with pit latrines was steadily increasing. For example, this table gives the percentage of the urban population in Zambia served by various systems.®

Iwugo et al, 1978b

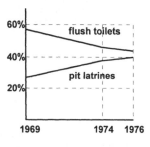

Facility	1969	1974	1976	
Flush toilet	56.7	46.2	43.9	decreasing
Aqua privy	7.0	5.4	4.8	decreasing
Pit latrines	26.7	37.7	40.1	increasing
Bucket latrines	2.1	1.5	1.3	decreasing
None	7.5	9.2	9.9	increasing

Sierra Leone, 1989

Misra, 1988

Wagner & Lanoix, 1958

In Freetown 87 per cent of households used pit latrines in 1989.® Most of Dar es Salaam's population use them. In India the twin pit pour-flush pit latrine is advocated for urban and rural people except in cities with a population of more than a hundred thousand (a lakh in India).

Archeologists at Vaishli in Bihar found pit latrines built about 500 BC with terracotta covers® and more than three million pit latrines (called 'privies')® were constructed in the United States in the 1930s.

Crude pits

In some places pit latrines have a bad reputation. Crude pits consisting of an open pit with logs or boards across the top are condemned because:

• the floor cannot be kept clean, leading to spread of

disease, especially hookworms;

- flies breed in the pit;
- mosquitoes (especially *Culex* mosquitoes) breed in wet pits;
- the pits are malodorous;
- children fall into the pit through gaps in the floor;
- the timber floor may be attacked by termites and may then collapse; and
- the sides of the pit fall in, leading to complete collapse of the whole latrine.

Fear of collapse is sometimes justified. In 1981 in Mbale in eastern Uganda, I heard that a woman had been killed when a latrine fell in. Recently a three-month-old baby in Kampala was rescued from a pit by a boy scout.® It is also recorded in England that in 1326 a man met his death in his own latrine when he fell through rotten planks and drowned 'monstrously in his own excrement'.®

New Vision, 1993

Lambton, 1978

In some countries latrines are considered to be dangerous because they are frequented by bad spirits.®

Kotolava, 1984

Satisfactory simple pit latrines

However, simple pits may be satisfactory if:

- the pit is deep and kept dark, so that it is unattractive to flies;
- the floor is smooth and impervious and is kept clean;
- the floor rests on a base which prevents surface water entering; and
- at least the top metre of the pit is lined to prevent collapse.

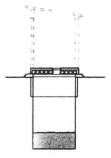

simple pit

The best soil for a pit is one that does not collapse whether it is dry or wet, but is also reasonably easy to dig. Pits can be satisfactory in other types of soil, provided suitable measures are taken. For example, loose soil can be supported by boards during excavation and by a lining later. Large stones or boulders can be broken up by lighting a fire to heat them and then pouring on water.® Hard solid rock is difficult to dig, but there are reports of people using explosives to break it up. Determined latrine builders excavate pits in what appear to be impossible conditions. Near Nairobi I saw a pit latrine excavated in hard rock in a disused stone quarry. The rock dug from the hole had been used to build the shelter. However, with fissured rock there

Langshaw, 1952

is a danger of pollution travelling rapidly and therefore travelling long distances.

Pit size and 'life'

The size of pit often recommended is about a metre across and three metres deep. A diameter of 900mm is common in some places, but where a spade is used it is difficult to dig a pit less than 1100mm across. ® Pits that are circular in plan are more stable than square or rectangular pits,® but are more difficult to dig. The bigger the pit, the longer it will last.

Brandberg, 1983

Franceys, Pickford & Reed, 1992

If a pit is small it will fill up with solids quickly. When water is used for flushing the pan, as in a water-seal latrine (Section 4e), the pit must also be big enough to allow liquid to infiltrate into the surrounding soil.

Pits should be taken out of use when the solids reach about half a metre below the top. Unless infiltration rates are a limiting factor (see below), the 'life' of a pit is the time it takes for solids to fill up to that level. There is obviously a direct relationship between:

- the 'life' of a pit;
- the rate of solids accumulation and
- the volume of the pit up to 500 mm below the top.

The rate of solids accumulation in a pit depends on:

- the number of people using the latrine;
- the amount of faeces each user excretes, which may vary with diet;
- the nature of the surrounding soil;
- the level of the groundwater; and
- the lining, if there is one;

and, especially important

- the material used for anal cleaning.

Methods of anal cleaning

In the Volta Region of Ghana a survey with 251 respondents showed that 23 per cent used newspaper and other paper, 22 per cent used corncobs, others used rags, stones, leaves or a combination of these. Only 2 per cent used water and 5 per cent toilet paper.® In Myanmar about a quarter of people use sticks.® According to the Koran, Muslims should use water for cleaning if it is available. Water is generally used in India.

Wright et al, 1978

Oo & Thwin, 1987

Rate of solids accumulation

As a rough guide, the rate of accumulation of solids may be taken as 40 litres per person per year (40 lpy) if water is used for anal cleaning and the pit is wet.

If the pit is dry, or if solid material such as grass, corncobs or newspaper is used for anal cleaning, 60 litres per person per year (60 lpy) may be assumed as the rate of solids accumulation. If solid anal cleaning material is used in a dry pit, 90 litres per person per year (90 lpy) may be assumed.

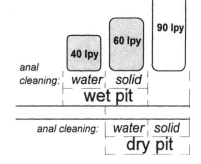

> I prefer 'person' to 'head' or 'capita' and so use quantities like *litres **per person** per year* (lpy) and *litres per person per day* (lpd) throughout this book.

Another recommendation makes no allowance for wet pits and allows for solid accumulation of 60 lpy (+ 50 per cent where bulky materials are used for anal cleaning). ®

Cairncross, 1988

These figures are conservative, as little reliable data is available. In Zimbabwe, where more than twenty thousand VIP latrines were constructed in the 1970s, it was found that in family units where water was added regularly and paper was used for anal cleaning, the rate of accumulation was sometimes as low as 20 lpy.® Pits are normally 3 metres deep and 1.5 metres to 1.75 metres in diameter.®

Morgan & Chimbunde, 1982
Morgan and Mara, 1982

In India the design of twin pits for pour-flush latrines (Section 4e) has a different basis.® Solids are retained for only two or three years and it is assumed that combined sludge and water fills the pit more quickly than when water is not used for anal cleaning and flushing. So a figure of 78.5 litres per person per year is used for wet pits. For a dry pit the recommended rate of solids accumulation is 40 lpy. I have not been able to discover why such a precise figure as 78.5 lpy is used. Perhaps it is due to engineers' liking for precision. Unnecessarily accurate dimensions are often given.®

Roy et al, 1984;
GOI/RWSG-SA, 1992

A study carried out in the early 1980s® suggested that it is better to estimate the accumulation of sludge on the basis of dry sludge rather than volume. The average figure then suggested was 12kg of dry matter per person per year. Compacted pit sludge in Africa has a moisture content around fifty or sixty per cent, giving a volume of 25 — 30 lpy. In Bangkok the sludge is much wetter, around 85 per cent moisture giving about 80 lpy, and in Japan and Taiwan

Pickford, 1985
Schertenleib & Hawkins, 1983

the nightsoil in vaults is about 97 per cent water, yielding about 400 lpy.

From this study it was also deduced that solids only start to accumulate at the bottom of a wet pit after about six months. Before that the decomposition of fresh faeces releases gas bubbles, lifting the sludge to form a scum.

It is likely that over several years consolidation results in a reducing rate of accumulation. The volume of sludge was measured in twelve pits in the Gangetic plain over periods up to seven and a half years.® The pits were 'wet' and water was used for anal cleaning. Recent analysis of the data gave a reasonable straight line equation for the total sludge volume in litres per person (*A*) after *y* years, where *y* is greater than three:

$$A = 150 + 6\,y.$$

Adhya & Saha, 1986

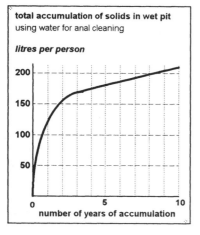

total accumulation of solids in wet pit using water for anal cleaning

litres per person

Shallow pits

Shallow trench pits are suitable for temporary use such as after disasters (floods, earthquakes and the like) where they are expected to be in use for only a few weeks. They are commonly 300mm wide and up to 1.5 metres deep. A length of about three metres is recommended for every hundred people. Excavated soil should be heaped beside the trench and used to cover faeces after each use — shovels used for digging are sometimes left by the latrine. When the trench is filled to about 300mm below ground level the latrine should be abandoned and the remaining heaped-up soil returned.® Pits about 300mm square by a metre deep are recommended for temporary use during cholera epidemics.® The pit should be coated with unslaked lime each day.

Assar, 1971

WHO, 1993a

Large pits

Pits in suitable soils may be very large. As part of an upgrading scheme for urban areas in Malawi® the volume of pits was increased to one cubic metre per user. The lifetime was expected to be between thirty and fifty years. I estimated that some latrines I examined in East Africa had already been used more than two hundred thousand times!

In Indonesia a UNDP sanitation project involving five hundred households found that householders were unhappy with the pits provided, which were about two metres deep and 800mm diameter — giving a volume of about one

Brandberg, 1988

cubic metre. Seventy per cent of householders enlarged their pits to an average four cubic metres. They also used permanent materials such as clay bricks for the pit lining, instead of the bamboo matting used for the small pits. Most of these enlarged pits are under the houses.®

de Kruijff, 1987

In Uganda rural pits are often about 0.6 metres wide, 1.2 metres long and four to eight metres deep.® They are usually dug by skilled professional diggers and are unsupported (unlined) in stable laterite. Usual depths reported are four to six metres in Sri Lanka® and nine metres in the Kizoma Region of Tanzania.®

Causer, 1993a

Abhayagoonawardhana, 1981
Kalimanzila, 1980

In Mbarara in 1981 I met a Ugandan, who I suppose was about 35 years old. He had just completed his latrine and told me it was 42 feet (12.8 metres) deep. I queried this and he assured me that it was certainly 42 feet deep. So I asked him why he had dug so deep a pit. His reply was immediate: 'because I want it to last me and my family for the rest of my life'. In a peri-urban area of Nairobi I saw what the contractor claimed was an even deeper pit — 50 feet (15.2 metres). This had been excavated for a beer hall and when completed would have a double latrine, two cubicles side by side.

Official recommendations in parts of East Africa require a depth of six or seven metres (eighteen or twenty feet).® Experience there® was that if pits were deeper than four metres they never filled up. In Juba it was found that ninety-five per cent of pit latrines were more than three metres deep, and eighty per cent were more than four metres. A quarter were more than five metres, the depth prescribed by the town council.® Some pits in Sudan are reported to be 25 metres deep.®

Tannahill, 1966
Duquehin, 1978; Railton, 1978

Nichols, 1982
Feachem , Maraet al, 1979

I was involved in a survey in Dar es Salaam that gave the volumes as shown here ⇒. I looked down many pits which had served their households for more than twenty years and were still in use with no nuisance from smell or flies.

A history of Oxfordshire, England, written by Robert Plot in 1677, mentions a college long house latrine. It was so 'large and deep that it has never been emptied since the foundation of the college', which was about 300 years previously.® Another latrine built in the middle ages in England was at St Albans Abbey. The depth of the pit below the cloister floor level was 25 feet (7.6 metres).®

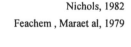
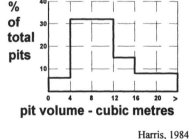

% of total pits

pit volume - cubic metres

Harris, 1984

Wright, 1960

large pits below small slabs

Adhya & Saha, 1986

Large cover slabs are expensive and if made of reinforced concrete require a lot of steel and cement. A large volume pit can be formed below a small slab by methods like those shown here ⇐. The method shown in the centre is known as 'corbelling' and is mentioned again on page 61.

Size for liquid infiltration

As well as providing sufficient capacity for the accumulation of solids, a pit must be large enough for infiltration of liquid into the surrounding soil. Little liquid results from the decomposition of faeces, but a pit may also receive up to a litre of urine per person per day and water used for washing the slab, water for flushing pour-flush pans and water used for anal cleaning. In some places latrines are used for bathing, either because it is the custom or for religious reasons. Sullage may also be put in a pit.

Liquid infiltrates from a pit into the soil around it at a rate that depends on the type of liquid, the type of soil and the level of the groundwater. Liquid from pits and septic tanks has a high load of microorganisms which block the pores between the soil particles. Percolation of sullage, which has fewer microorganisms, is usually faster.

When a pit penetrates groundwater, the liquid level inside the pit builds up above the level of the groundwater. This gives a 'hydraulic gradient' that pushes liquid out of the pit. Tests near Calcutta® showed that the difference of liquid level inside and outside the pit gradually increases as the pores between the soil particles become blocked.

For percolation into soils in the unsaturated zone (above the groundwater) the long term infiltration capacity in litres per square metre per day may be taken as follows

soil type	pits and septic tanks	soakaways for sullage
sands	50	200
silts and loams	30	100
clays	10 or less	50 or less

Sand particles are larger than 0.05mm, clay particles smaller than 0.002mm, and silt lies between. Some clays which expand when wet have such low infiltration capacities that they are unsuitable for pour-flush latrine pits. Because infiltration of liquid into rock is slow, pits dug in rock need to be large, even though the excavation is difficult. If rock is fractured, water from pits may travel quickly, leading to groundwater pollution far away.

There are contrary views about whether sullage should be put into pit latrines, which are discussed in Chapter 8.

b. Control of flies, mosquitoes and smell

The most common complaints about unsatisfactory latrines refer to nuisance from bad smells, flies and mosquitoes. All the respondents in a survey of 27 projects in Yemen complained about the smell from their existing latrines.® In Juba, Sudan, nearly half the pit latrine owners said 'smell' was their chief complaint.®

Mullick, 1987

Nichols, 1982

Flies are also one of the most important agents for the transmission of faeces-derived diseases. Flies like to feed on faeces and the females lay their eggs on faeces, to which they are attracted by smell. Thousands of newly-hatched flies may emerge from open pits, carrying particles of faeces to their next meal, which may be human food.

Whether a pit is dry or wet seems to make no difference to fly breeding, but mosquitoes only breed in wet pits as the larvae need water to swim in and a free liquid surface for their breathing siphon.® Therefore an important consideration in providing good pit latrines is limiting the access of flies and mosquitoes to the pit and preventing their escape from the pit. It is a bonus if unpleasant smells are also controlled.

Curtis & Hawkins, 1982

There is usually little bother with pits that are deep and dark. Even for comparatively shallow pits these three methods are effective for control of these nuisances:

- **tight-fitting lids over squat holes** — see Section (4c);
- **vertical vents with flyproof netting at the top** — see Sections (4d); and
- **water seals between latrine pans and pits** — see Section (4e).

Some methods of controlling flies, mosquitoes and smell in existing latrines are described in Section 8c. These include putting a floating layer of polystyrene beads in a flooded pit. Female mosquitoes cannot lay eggs and the larvae cannot breathe through the layer of beads, so it is effective in mosquito control.

c. Pits with lids

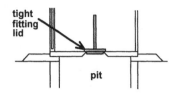

Iwugo *et al*, 1978a

Alvarinho, 1991

seat with hinged lid

Wagner & Lanoix, 1958

Brandberg, 1988

Causer, 1993b

Brandberg, 1993

Pazlar, 1994

IRC Newsletter, 1993

One method of dealing with flies and smells is to place a lid over the squat hole whenever the hole is not in use. A simple lid consists of a board slightly larger than the hole with a handle or a piece of cord to lift it.

Inspection in 1978 of pit latrines in the inner core area of Ibadan, which served at least fifty thousand people, found that wooden covers were normally used to close the squat holes.®

Good latrine seats have a lid that is hinged at the back. If it fits tightly, the lid effectively controls flies and smell.

Lids are claimed to have been very successful in controlling flies in Mozambique, where fifty thousand household latrines with unreinforced dome slabs and concrete lids were built in the 1980s.® Experience elsewhere has not been so good. In the 1950s it was claimed that 'no case has been reported where covers have been successfully used and kept in place over a period of months or years. Even in the USA, where people in general are conscious of sanitation, the problem of seat covers has not been solved'.®

A type of latrine that has become popular in parts of Africa has a removable concrete lid. The lid is cast in the squat hole of a concrete slab. This ensures that the lid fits tightly in the hole.® Flies and cockroaches cannot get in or out of the pit when the lid is in position.

In one design a concrete slab which is supported by a traditional pole and mud floor. The slab, called a SanPlat, is 600mm square and 50mm thick. It weighs 30-35 kg so is easily lifted by two people. Women in Malawi, where the SanPlat was first used, often carry loads of firewood weighing more than 35kg. The SanPlat has a hard and smooth surface sloping towards the squat hole for easy cleaning, a keyhole shaped squat hole and footrests.

This type of slab was in use in Uganda in the early 1960s.® Its popularity increased in several countries in the 1980s. SanPlats are being introduced in Bangladesh®, Sierra Leone® and elsewhere. A project in Malawi trained village contractors to cast SanPlats with the aim of fifty per cent coverage of households.®

A latrine with a SanPlat is much cheaper than the VIP latrine described below. A VIP requires a building that is fairly dark inside, a vent and corrosion-resistant netting. A latrine with a tight-fitting cover only needs a screen for privacy.® However, when lids are used for public, communal or institutional latrines the handles are reported to become dirty, and therefore likely to spread disease.®

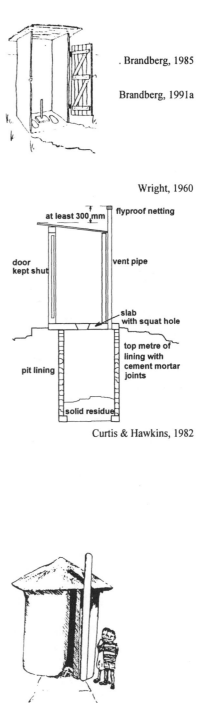

. Brandberg, 1985

Brandberg, 1991a

d. Ventilated pits

Ventilating pipes are used in many countries to remove unpleasant smells and flies from pits. The idea of venting pits is not new. An account for house repairs in 1450® includes 'makynge a vente for a privey to voyd yr heyr' [making a vent for a privy to void the air].

Wright, 1960

In the 1970s the Blair Laboratory in Zimbabwe developed the idea further and called the latrine the Blair latrine. It was much publicized by international agencies as the 'ventilated improved pit' (VIP) latrine.

The shelter for a VIP latrine must be kept fairly dark. Flyproof netting at the top of the vent pipe stops flies and mosquitoes getting in to or out from the pit, although flies are attracted to the vent top by the smell there. Any flies that hatch in the pit try to move towards light. If the shelter is fairly dark the flies go towards the top of the vent, because during daytime light is brighter at the vent top than in the shelter. The flies cannot escape because of the flyproof netting and eventually die.® Doors of rectangular latrines should be kept shut, but shelters with spiral walls are dark enough inside to make a door unnecessary.

Curtis & Hawkins, 1982

Wind passing across the top of the pipe causes an updraught which removes bad smells from the latrine and encourages flies to move towards the light. If the latrine is sited where there is no wind, the pipe may be put on the sunny side of the latrine and the outside of the pipe painted black, unless the pipe itself is black. Air in the pipe is then heated by the sun and rises, ventilating the pit.

To ensure that there is a flow of air through the latrine there must be adequate ventilation of the shelter. This is usually achieved by leaving openings above and below the door, or by using a spiral shelter without a door. If possible the entrance should face the prevailing wind.

A spiral-shaped shelter was introduced in Zimbabwe. The spiral is dark inside and needs no door, which saves money. The walls may be made of timber, bamboo, mud, ferrocement, or by spreading layers of cement mortar on hessian (sackcloth) supported by a bamboo frame. Rectangular spirals can be built with bricks or blocks.

The effectiveness of VIP latrines in controlling fly nuisance was demonstrated in Zimbabwe. Four pit latrines were built in a row. Two had vent pipes, two did not. They were all used equally for six months and then for two and a half months flies were trapped as they emerged from the squat holes. Nearly fourteen thousand flies were trapped in the unvented pits, but only 146 in the vented ones.®

Morgan, 1977

Permanent VIPs

Permanent VIPs can be built with a single pit or a double pit. In double VIP latrines the compartments are filled and emptied alternately as described in Section 4f, so they are sometimes called 'alternating' VIP latrines.®

Lochery & Adu-Asah, no date
Morgan, 1988

The 'tank and soakaway' version® consists of a watertight tank that overflows to a soakaway. The tank is desludged when solids occupy about three-quarters of the liquid volume of the tank. A long life can also be ensured by providing a large pit with an ordinary VIP latrine. Pits for VIP latrines in Sudan are usually 2.5 metres by 1.5 metres and between five and seven metres deep.®

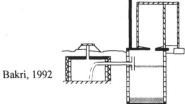

Bakri, 1992

Pickford, 1992

Vents

The vent® is ideally black plastic (uPVC) 150mm diameter pipe. This is expensive and may be difficult to obtain. Alternatives include asbestos cement pipes, galvanized iron, bamboo and mud. Reeds or hessian covered with cement mortar can be used for a 'home-made' pipe.® For a still cheaper version® old plastic bags are tied round a tube of reeds. Grass is tied round the outside to protect the plastic.

Ryan & Mara, 1983
Morgan, 1994

Instead of using a pipe, a vent may be incorporated in the shelter walls like a chimney stack. Vents of this kind are built with bricks, concrete or sandcrete blocks, or masonry. They may be placed outside or in the corner of the shelter. In Tanzania® special blocks with a 150mm diameter hole were made of quarry dust and cement.

Boydell, 1983

The vent should rise from the top of the pit (the underside of the cover slab) and should go at least 300mm above the highest part of a sloping roof. Some experts recommend taller vents, such as 450mm or 600mm above the roof.® Vent pipes are often not high enough with the top only level with or just above the roof. With a conical roof the vent should extend as high as the apex of the roof.

The internal size of the vent depends on the material of which it is made. It has been recommended that smooth pipes should be at least 100mm diameter, cement-rendered reed or hessian at least 200mm diameter. Chimney-type vents need to be 150mm square or more. Larger sizes are advised where there is little wind.

It is reported that some Tanzanian villagers made vent pipes with bush sticks cemented with cow dung. ® These were placed at the inside end of the spiral mud walls, which was also the apex of the roof. The part of the vent above the roof (also made of sticks and dung) was effective as a fly screen and gave good ventilation of the pit.

In some places vent pipes are fixed at the bottom but have no support higher up. They are then liable to damage. Apart from being convenient to fix clothes lines, a vent pipe provides a lovely target for football shooting or stumps for cricket. Pipes should therefore be supported near the top of the latrine wall by a strong bracket.

Flyproof netting must be fixed at the top of the vent. In Mozambique® galvanized steel mesh corroded in a few weeks. PVC-coated glass fibre netting may be attacked by cockroaches. Even without their attention it only lasts about five years. So if possible the netting should be made of stainless steel or aluminium. A mesh size that is often recommended is 1mm by 1.5mm.

The top of a chimney-type vent built of bricks or blocks sometimes has a raised edge as shown in the top drawings here. This reduces the suction due to wind passing across the top. It may also collect leaves, obstructing the ventilation. So the top should be made like the lower drawing here.

Netting is sometimes made into a cone or dome on top of the vent. This is unsatisfactory as it reduces the updraught — the netting should be flat. Another unsatisfactory variation is to put little roofs over vents to prevent rain entering. For one latrine I saw in Ghana the builder thought he had a good idea by making bends at the top, like ventilators on ships. These modifications ignore the need for flies inside a pit to see daylight at the top of the vent if the VIP is to work properly.

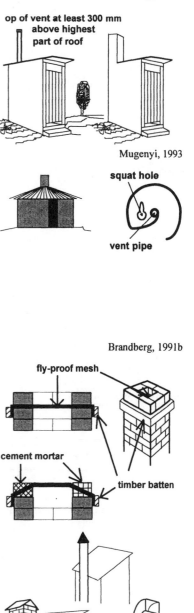

Mara, 1994; Brandberg, 1991b

op of vent at least 300 mm above highest part of roof

Mugenyi, 1993

squat hole

vent pipe

Brandberg, 1991b

fly-proof mesh

cement mortar

timber batten

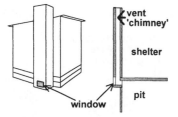

Morgan & Clarke, 1978

Unrau, 1978

Goss, 1992

Swaffield & Wakelin, 1988,
  Wakelin et al, 1987

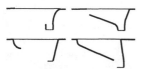

sections of common pans

When existing pit latrines were changed to VIPs in Malawi 'chimneys' were built outside the shelters. so that the slabs could be left. Flies were attracted by glass windows fitted opposite openings in the pit lining. They could be seen coming out from the pit and then (seeing daylight at the top of the vent) they flew upwards.

Watergate bowls

The Watergate was introduced for those who like to defecate into water, as in a WC. The bowl filled from a tank automatically and the contents discharged into the pit below.® Ten Watergates were tried in St Lucia and worked well.® Like all mechanical devices, the 'Watergate' was liable to go wrong and rarely lasted as long as the pit.

e. Water seal latrines

A study in Sierra Leone® found many disadvantages with VIP latrines, so water-seal latrines were adopted for people who used water for anal cleaning.

A WC, whether of the sit-down or squatting type, has a water seal and is flushed with water from a cistern. It therefore needs a piped water supply and usually discharges to a sewerage system or septic tank (see Chapter 6). Although low-volume cisterns and WCs have been developed®, the usual flush is at least nine litres. Both capital and operational costs are high.

A low-cost alternative is a pour-flush latrine. A well-designed pan and trap can be cleaned by carefully pouring one to one-and-a-half litres of water from a jar or other vessel. Pans with a smooth surface that cleans easily are made with GRP, plastic or glazed earthenware. In south Asia I have seen excellent pans made of concrete or cement mortar finished with marble chips that are polished with carborundum stone. Experience indicates that the base of a pan should have a slope of at least 25° to make sure solids are washed away..

A pour-flush latrine is suitable where water is brought from a pond, well, yard-tap or public standpipe. If water is in short supply, or has to be carried very long distances, sullage (waste water that has already been used for bathing or washing pots and pans) can be used for flushing. However, greasy water can make pans hard to clean.

Pour-flush latrines are also favoured by some people who use soft paper for anal cleaning. For example, low-volume pedestal pour-flush units are used in Columbia and Brazil. ® Pour-flush latrines are often blocked where leaves, newspaper and similar hard material is used for anal cleaning. Sometimes this material is put aside for later burial or burning, but then attracts flies.

UNCHS, 1984

The water seal

Where the pit is below the latrine, a simple water seal (sometimes called a 'gooseneck' trap) can be made with a hemispherical bowl below a vertical outlet to the pan.

A survey in Sri Lanka villages found that many gooseneck traps were not used. Some traps had been accidentally broken, but the most common reason was lack of flushing water.® In 1992 nearly half the water seals in an area of Bangladesh had been intentionally broken to make the pan easier to clean and to avoid blockage.®

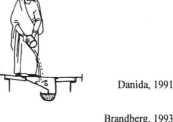

Danida, 1991

Brandberg, 1993

More often the trap is made with a U-bend in the outlet pipe. Traps for pour-flush are best with easy bends (no sharp turns). Seals can be much shallower than the usual WC trap and are usually 15mm to 25mm deep. Variations in the design of pans and traps have been developed in many countries including India, Malaysia, the New Hebrides, the Philippines and at Chiangmai in Thailand.®

shallow water seal trap

UNCHS, 1984

A P-trap is usual when the pan discharges through a sloping pipe or channel to an offset pit. The pour-flush can then be inside a house with the pit outside, although more often the pan is in a latrine shelter that is separate from the house. A 75mm or 100mm pipe or a cement-lined covered channel conveys excreta and water to the pit. The outlet of the pipe or channel should extend about 200mm into the pit to prevent accumulation of solids on one side.

Pour-flush latrines were introduced in India by the All India Institute of Hygiene and Public Health in 1943. Twin pit versions described in Section 4f followed in 1958 and pour-flush latrines were used for urban areas from 1967.®

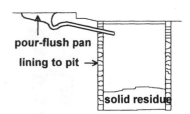

pour-flush pan

lining to pit →

solid residue

World Water,1983

Over five thousand pedestal-type pour-flush latrines were installed in Fiji.® They consisted of a 3mm thick polythene bowl and seal made in New Zealand and a precast concrete riser.

An ingenious modification of the offset pour-flush latrine suitable for places where water is seasonally in short

Rao, 1976

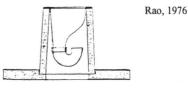

supply was suggested from Malaysia. The pan is flushed into the pit in the usual way when water is plentiful. During the dry season a squat hole can be opened in the three-section pit cover and the latrine used without water.®

f. Full pits and twin pits

Pits are usually taken out of use when the contents reach about half a metre below the top. Then they are filled with soil to ground level or above. A practice in Uganda and Nigeria, and probably many other countries, is to plant a banana tree on the site of a filled pit.® The tree benefits from the decomposing humus and prevents people falling into the old pit as it sinks.

In some places bulky solids such as corncobs are used for anal cleaning and are then put in the pit, which obviously fills more quickly. So it is sensible to put them in a box or basket for separate burial or burning. In Mashonaland, Zimbabwe, corncobs are often dropped into pits. It is common practice to pour several litres of paraffin or diesel oil into prematurely full pits and to drop in a lighted match to burn up the corncobs. There have been accidents and sometimes an explosion 'like a bomb'.®

So that people are not without a latrine, a new pit should be dug before the old one fills. Floor slabs and shelters may be moved to the second pit if they are made of suitable materials.

Manual emptying of pits

As an alternative to digging a new pit, a pit may be emptied. The practice of manually emptying single pits as soon as they are full involves serious health hazards. Some of the excreta is fresh, smelly and attractive to flies, apart from containing living faecal organisms that may transmit disease. Nevertheless, manual emptying is quite usual. In 1992 WEDC sent questionnaires to about 300 people worldwide. Replies gave information about a wide range of matters concerned with latrines and septic tanks.® Over 40 per cent of respondents reported that all or most of pits in their areas were emptied manually.

In some villages in Bangladesh nearly all household pits are emptied when they become full.® Most people pay scavengers to do this unpleasant work. Only three per cent

Syarikat Gibson Perniagaan, no date

Harrison, 1987

Maramah, 1990

.Pickford, 1993

Chadha & Strauss, 1991

of households dig new pits.

In some places there is keen competition amongst contractors to secure latrine emptying business. In Dar es Salaam, householders like the personal contact with contractors, which contrasts with the bureaucratic system of emptying by council tankers. Prices can be negotiated and the householder can choose the day for starting the work.® Elsewhere there is a stigma attached to the work. In Malindi in Kenya labourers are so ashamed to do the work that they always empty pits at night when they are not recognized. One official service and seven private companies empty pits.®

Muller et al, 1993

Malombe, 1993

One system used for emptying is to dig another pit near to the latrine pit. In the island of Lamu off the Kenyan coast this has been practised for generations The 'temporary' hole is dug in the road right against the outside of the latrine pit lining and goes down as deep as the pit. Some lining blocks near the bottom are taken out so that the solids in the latrine pit flow into the hole. More solid material is shovelled out. Then the hole is topped up with soil and the road is reinstated.

England et al, 1980

Somewhat similar methods are used in Tanzania®, Sierra Leone and Nigeria, although usually a shallow hole is dug a few metres from the pit and solids are dug out from the top of the pit. The pit contents are black and foul. When topping-up the hole old bicycle frames and other rubbish are sometimes dumped on top of the excreta.

Muller et al, 1993

In Sekoto in northern Nigeria the slab is pushed aside or the squat hole is enlarged and then ash in put in the pit, followed by disinfectant and kerosene. A trench is dug in the compound near to the latrine and the pit contents are transferred to the trench by buckets. Finally the trench is back-filled with excavated soil.®

Garban, 1990

Mechanical emptying of pits

Where suitable equipment is available, lined pits can be emptied mechanically. Some accumulated solids may be lifted by jetting with water or agitating the contents with the end of the suction hose. Ordinary vacuum tankers used for emptying septic tanks and road gulleys are generally not powerful enough to completely empty pits. Pit solids in southern Africa® had densities over 2000kg per cubic metre. A pit is easier to empty mechanically if the contents

Developing World Water, 1988

are wet (e.g. a VIP latrine with soakaway).

In June 1990 a tanker was purchased by KWAHO, a large and successful Kenyan NGO, for emptying pits in Kibera, the largest informal settlement in Nairobi. At first KWAHO collected fees for emptying but the project collapsed in January 1993 because operators retained fees and no funds were available for vehicle maintenance.®

Munyakho, 1994

The 'Brevac' tanker was designed specifically for pit emptying.® It has a high-performance liquid ring pump and large sludge capacity. In tests in Gaborone a Brevac lifted the heaviest sludge (with 80 per cent solids) over 64 metres through a 100mm diameter hose. However, these tankers are expensive and are so large that manoeuvring in congested urban areas is difficult or impossible.

Carroll, 1985

Smaller, cheaper, slower and more manoeuvrable tractor-type tankers have been developed.® Their slow speed ensures a long life, but restricts the operating distance. Other tankers are mounted on four-wheel-drive vehicles. Using engines and pumps that are locally used for other purposes increases the likelihood that spare parts and skills for maintenance are available.

Coffey, 1988

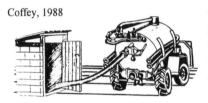

At an even smaller scale, a manually-operated pump was developed in the Netherlands for trials in Dar es Salaam.®It uses a vacuum to transfer pit contents to 200-litre oil drums and is particularly suitable for operation by the informal sector. Small groups of men who have been trained to use the apparatus work independently, making their own arrangements with householders.

Rijnsburger, 1991, Muller et al, 1993

Alternating pits

A long life for a pit latrine can be obtained by constructing two lined pits that are used alternately. The accumulated solid in one pit (or part of a divided pit) is left long enough to become inoffensive before it is removed. One of the 'twin' pits (pit **A**) is used for two or three years. When it is nearly full, it is sealed and the second pit (pit **B**) is put into use. Solids taken from pits that have been out of use for two years resemble soil, have no unpleasant smell and are free from pathogens, even the long-living roundworm eggs. As the pits only need a short life (two or three years) they can be comparatively shallow. Then the decomposed solids can easily be taken out by householders or contractors.

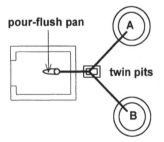

When separate twin pits are used with pour-flush

latrines, a Y-junction is usually built in an access chamber. One branch of the Y is blocked while the other branch is open to allow excreta to pass to the pit. This type of latrine is very common in the Indian sub-continent.

In most soils it is necessary to provide pits with linings if they are emptied. Without a lining the sides of the pit are likely to collapse. Linings are discussed in Section 4g.

At first many people are reluctant to dig decomposed excreta, even through it is harmless and does not smell bad. There are often local taboos or religious laws prohibiting contact with 'unclean' material. Elsewhere people have gradually become aware of the value of decomposed excreta as a fertilizer.

Double pits

Instead of completely separate twin pits, a single pit can be divided into two, sometimes called a 'double pit'. The dividing wall between the two chambers should have a good foundation and should extend at least to the outside of the lining. It should be fully mortared on both sides to prevent seepage from the chamber in use getting into the 'resting chamber'. In India I was told by A.K.Roy, one of the best-known advocates of pour-flush latrines, that the sludge in the 'resting' chambers of double pit latrines often remain wet and faecal micro-organisms migrate from the chamber in use to the resting chamber.

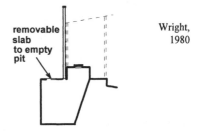

well built dividing wall extending beyond lining

The KVIP ('K' because it was first used in Kumasi in Ghana) is an emptiable VIP. Early studies in Ghana® showed that it is better to slope the inner wall at 60 degrees to the horizontal rather than using a vertical wall. Double pits with seats are popular in some countries. Section 10d describes multi-compartment alternating VIPs. In many places this type of latrine is used for institutional and public latrines.

removable slab to empty pit

Wright, 1980

Other designs used in southern Africa were the RIP (raised improved pit) and the VIDP ® (ventilated improved double pit latrine). With all double VIP latrines either both chambers have vent pipe or collars. With collars a vent pipe is fitted above the compartment in use and a plug in the other collar. Both are jointed with weak mortar.

The total cost of double-pit VIP latrines in Lesotho was found to be almost the same as single pits over a twenty year period. This is because removal and disposal of sludge

Nostrand & Wilson, 1983

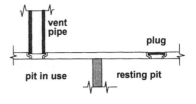

vent pipe

plug

pit in use   resting pit

Read, 1980

from single pits is more expensive, as shown below.®

Costs relative to construction of single pit	construction (excluding shelter)	emptying (Net present value)	TOTAL
Single pit	100	37.7	137.7
Double pit	134.6	5.4	140.0

Experience of twin and double pits

Because of hard rock at shallow depth in the inner core area of Ibadan there was a tradition of digging pits in pairs.®

Iwugo et al, 1978a

When a pit was emptied the contents were usually put on the ground around the pit.

Bakhteari & Wegelin-Schuringa, 1992

The first manual emptying of a double pit in the Baldia sanitation project in Karachi® caused a lot of interest. It had been left for over a year. It was reported that 'excitement was high as none of the project team and none of the masons or community members had ever seen dried-out pit contents . . When the contents were dug up, they formed a sort of dry cake without any smell and not in the least offensive. Word about this spread through the communities and helped enormously in the acceptance of the double pit design'.

However, some of the double pits were badly built, with a gap left between the dividing wall and the lining. I saw several built in this way. The contents of the 'resting chamber' would then not dry out.

gap between dividing wall and lining in double pit in Karachi

From 1979 onwards many thousands of double pit VIPs were constructed in Botswana, most in sites and services development. There has been much misuse, particularly by putting sullage into the pits, resulting in over-wet sludge. Even so, faecal organisms are reduced by several orders of magnitude, although even in well-run double pits some pathogens remained after a year.®

Wheeler & Carroll, 1989

g. Slabs and linings

Slabs

For a pit beneath a latrine, the slab acts as the cover of the pit and the floor on which users put their feet. So it must be strong enough to support the user. To check that slabs are strong enough, with a 'factor of safety', concrete slabs are sometimes tested by getting five men to stand on them.

The pit of a pour-flush latrine can be completely offset and the latrine floor can be supported on firm ground. The necessary strength of pit covers depends on their position. If under roads they must not collapse under the heaviest vehicles. Normally slabs must be able to carry people walking or standing on them.

Cover slabs are commonly made of concrete, which is durable and can be cleaned easily. Where termite-resistant timber is available, the slab can be made of logs. In some countries logs are soaked in used engine oil to discourage termites.

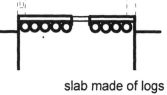

slab made of logs covered with a layer of mud

Log slabs are often covered with a layer of mud. Local traditional methods (such as mixing soil with liquid made by soaking cow dung or cassava in water) can be used to give a mud floor a smooth surface. Boards, bamboo and metal sheets are also used. Exceptionally a brick or masonry arch is built.

A flat slab, such as one made of reinforced concrete, needs proper support at its edges. If the pit is not lined the slab needs about 200mm support all round. So for a 1100mm diameter pit the slab should be 1500mm diameter. When resting on a firm base, such as the top of a brick lining or a concrete ring, 50mm wide support may be enough, giving a 1200mm diameter slab for a 1100mm diameter pit.

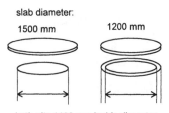

slab diameter:
1500 mm   1200 mm

both pits 1100 mm inside diameter

As well as supporting the slab, the base prevents hookworm larvae getting out and insects or small animals getting in or out, provided the joint between base and slab is properly sealed. Bases are made of brick, masonry or termite resistant logs. A good base can be made before the pit is dug by digging a shallow trench round a circle marked out for the pit and filling it with concrete, puddled clay or stabilized soil. Raising the top of a base above ground level and forming a bank with excavated soil prevents surface water entering a pit. Roof water (whether or not it is collected in gutters) should be channelled away from pits.

Slabs made of concrete reinforced with steel bars or wire mesh can be prefabricated. A satisfactory slab® one metre in diameter is 50mm thick at the outside with a slope towards the squat hole where the thickness is 40mm. Circular prefabricated slabs have the advantage that they can be moved by rolling. For large pits the slab may be

Franceys,
Pickford &
Reed, 1992

made in two or more sections. Joints should be sealed with nud or cement mortar, to prevent flies, mosquitoes and cockroaches getting in or out.

Ferrocement slabs

Boydell, 1983

Slabs reinforced with chicken wire have been made thinner, lighter and easier to handle than reinforced concrete slabs. ® In Tanzania I examined some slabs only 18 mm thick that had been in use for two years without trouble. They had three layers of chicken wire, which was extravagant; two layers are usual. Ferrocement slabs were tried in Mozambique, but all failed under test. This was probably because it is difficult to compact concrete properly with two layers of chicken wire in the middle. Chicken wire is also expensive and is often difficult to obtain.® Moreover, there may be 'customer resistance' by users for whom a thin slab looks unsafe.

Brandberg, 1983

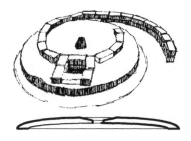

section of Mozambique slab

Paqui, 1988

Brandberg, 1994

Domed slabs

Concrete slabs without any reinforcement can be made as thin flat domes. This ensures that all the concrete is under compression when the user stands or squats on the slab. Domed slabs are simply made and are lighter than conventional reinforced slabs. They were originally developed in Mozambique in 1979 and proved popular there and in other parts of southern Africa. By 1988 more than 25 000 slabs had been made in Mozambique and demand far exceeded the supply.®

Standard sizes are 1.2 metres and 1.5 metres diameter. ® The top of the concrete slopes to the outside except for 100 mm around the squat hole, where it slopes inwards. The outwards slope has the disadvantage that water spilled or used for washing the floor makes the bottom of the shelter walls wet. This is particularly troublesome for shelters with mud walls.

Removable slabs

When a pit is to be emptied, either manually or by vacuum tanker, the whole or part of the slab should be removable. A common practice is to lower tankers' suction pipes through squat holes. This often damages the sides of the hole. If the damage is not made good, squat holes and slabs are hard to keep clean, encouraging hookworm infection.

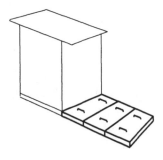

Removable slabs have handles (usually made of reinforcing steel) for easy lifting and should be sealed with weak mortar to ensure an insect-proof joint. Mortar made with mud or lime is suitable. Small slabs, such as those used for offset twin pits, may be light enough to be lifted by two men. For large slabs made in sections, the removable section should be at least 600mm wide. This allows a suction pipe to be moved around so that all the contents are taken out and can be seen to be taken out.

Squat holes, footrests and seats

Unless a latrine has a water seal or seat, a squat hole is formed in the slab. Excreta falls through the hole to the pit below. I have seen many different shapes in Africa, of which these are examples.

squat hole shapes

A hole about 400mm long prevents fouling of the slab by faeces and urine. Children are unlikely to fall into the pit if the hole is not wider than 180mm. A 'keyhole' shape is often used.

Except for domed slabs, the top of the slab should slope towards the hole. Then spilled water, or water used for cleaning, drains to the pit. A slope of 1 in 5 around the hole and 1 in 20 over the rest of the floor has been recommended.® Painting with two coats of 5 per cent solution of water glass (silicate of soda) is reputed to prevent concrete absorbing urine.

Brandberg, 1991a

Footrests are often provided with both squat holes and pour-flush pans. Footrests are usually about 100mm high, made of concrete. They keep the feet above the floor and help users to be comfortable when squatting. They help the user to find the right position even at night, reducing the chance of fouling the slab.

The best position of the footrests relative to the squat hole or pan depends on the posture adopted locally for defecating. The posture for defecation is an example of a cultural factor that may have an important influence on acceptability of latrines.

Where people prefer to sit rather than squat while defecating, a seat about 450 mm above the floor may be built over part of the pit. The seat is usually made of timber, with timber boards below the front of the seat down to the floor. Plastic seats with hinged covers are also available and sometimes seats are made of concrete or stone.

Pit linings

Unless the soil is stable when both dry and wet, a lining should always be provided. Whether the soil is stable or not, it is desirable to line the top half metre or so and to make this impervious to prevent surface water entering the pit or polluted liquid escaping by laying bricks or blocks with cement mortar joints. A lining with a strong top also provides a base for the cover slab. Alternatively, large stones reinforced with cement mortar can be made into a 'ring beam'.®

Old 200 litre oil drums have often been used for linings. In Myanmar® linings were made from several drums placed on top of each other. One end was left on the uppermost drum and a 300mm square squat hole was cut in it.

The lower part of a lining (below a metre or so) should allow liquid to infiltrate into the soil. Holes are made in metal sheets and oil drums. Sometimes holes are made in concrete pipes during manufacture, or are punched through after casting. Bricks, masonry and blocks are made with open joints and are often laid as a honeycomb unless the soil is too loose. A disadvantage of honeycomb construction is that it may provide access to the pit for rodents.® If soil is so loose that it runs through open vertical joints, the lining can be backed with 100mm of fine gravel.

In Tanzania various types of blocks were tested for suitability as pit linings®. They were immersed in the first chamber of a septic tank for 30 days. After this time blocks made of soil/cement mixture and sun dried mud blocks had completely collapsed.

Termite-resistant timber and bamboo may be used for linings in areas where they are plentiful. Softwood timber often rots in a few years and is also liable to attack by termites. Bamboo linings are sometimes pre-fabricated and complete linings are lowered into pits.

Circular pits can be lined by stacking blocks to form a ring that is stable and needs no mortar but which allows liquid to infiltrate into the soil.® A special type of block was devised by the UK Building Research Establishment.® Normal rectangular-shaped blocks are more usual. In Karachi I encouraged linings for large pits made with standard blocks (450mm x 225mm x 150mm). Fourteen

Morgan, 1994

Wilson, 1978

Ribeiro, 1985

Mowforth & Aggarwal, 1985

Brandberg, 1983
Carroll & Ashall, 1989

blocks made a ring in lower parts of pits. The tops of the linings were corbelled by gradually reducing the number of blocks in a ring. Corbelling can be used with blocks, bricks or masonry. A small cover slab is then required, often with considerable saving of cement, steel reinforcement and cost.

Sometimes linings are made too well because builders do not understand the importance of infiltration. In many villages of the Punjab sanitation programme in Pakistan soakpits were lined with bricks with cement joints. This not only reduced soakage; it added to the cost.® In Dar es Salaam I noticed two pits being lined with locally-quarried stone. One was jointed with cement mortar and the other had the stone bedded in clay. Both pits would be watertight and would therefore act as vaults rather than pits.

corbelling

Pasha & McGarry, 1989

Pits without linings

Pits without linings are stable up to seven or eight metres deep in sandy matrix, such as occurs in Jordan and Iran.® However, in Malawi two people were killed when the unlined pit they were digging collapsed. On investigation it was found that they had dug to a depth of twenty metres. ®

In moderately stable soils walls can be plastered with 10mm thick cement mortar. It may be reinforced with chicken wire.® Seepage holes should be left in the mortar to allow infiltration.

Wilson, 1978

Wegelin-Schuringa, 1991

Cairncross, 1988

h. Other pit latrines

Most pit latrines are of the types already described. Other types have been developed locally or are suitable for special conditions.

For example, offset pour-flush latrines without traps but with straight-through pipes have proved satisfactory in Myanmar, where some people use sticks for anal cleaning. They are the most popular form of sanitation in many parts of the country.® If vent pipes are provided, the latrines are like VIPs. I examined many latrines of this type in 1991. None was creating any nuisance from smell, flies or mosquitoes.

The ROEC (Reed's Odourless Earth Closet)® sold in southern Africa in the 1970s had a wide-mouthed asbestos cement chute. Owners complained that the chutes were

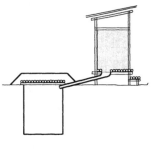

Rosenhall, 1990
Oo & Thwin,

Bestobell, 1944

difficult to keep clean and flies were a nuisance. I noticed a lot of faeces in the chutes of ROECs examined in Botswana. Brushes had been used for cleaning some chutes. When standing in the corner the dirty brushes proved a great attraction for flies. Another disadvantage of ROECs is the need for large quantities of water® for cleaning.The chutes also allow rodents to get into pits.®

UNCHS, 1982

Jeeyaseelen et al, 1987

Most houses in Bhutan have three floors - the ground floor for cattle; the first floor for the family's living space and the second floor for storage of grain and other crops. A balcony extends around the first floor and it is usual to defecate over the balcony at the rear. Under a latrine programme 100mm — 150mm PVC pipes were installed from balconies through holes in floors to pits below. Some of the latrines have vent pipes from the pits to above the roofs.®

Kai, 1990

Borehole latrines

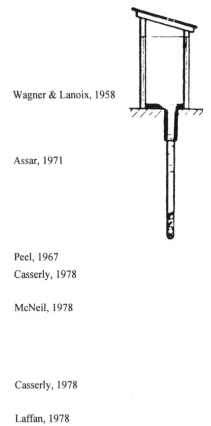

Borehole latrines, or 'bored hole latrines', can be excavated by manually operated augers or mechanical drills in firm soil that is free from rock or boulders. Diameters of 300mm to 400mm and depths up to ten metres are common.

Wagner & Lanoix, 1958

Augers can be made from 38 mm iron piping.® Village blacksmiths can easily make augers if shown what to do. Tripods and augers are sometimes included in kits prepared for disasters as boreholes can be dug quickly in an emergency.®

Assar, 1971

It is often claimed that boreholes soon fill and walls become fouled, leading to fly nuisance. Caving in of the walls may be a serious disadvantage. However, borehole latrines have been quite satisfactory in many places. Costs are low and in reasonably porous soil the bore has a long life.® Some have lasted five years.® Boreholes 500 mm in diameter and five metres deep were dug near Jos in Nigeria, and lasted fifty men for a year. There was no smell and few flies.®

Peel, 1967

Casserly, 1978

McNeil, 1978

The best diameter has been found to be about 400 mm, which is large enough to provide reasonable storage volume and to avoid fouling. Larger diameters are difficult to dig. Linings have been made of wood, cement, baked clay, galvanized iron and bamboo.® Pipes can be used for linings; pipes 300 mm diameter and three metres long were used in Malaysia. The auger could pass through the pipes.®

Casserly, 1978

Laffan, 1978

In Barmer district of Rajasthan boreholes 250mm in diameter were drilled to depths between ten and fifteen metres in an area about ten metres by six metres fenced off with dry bushes. Their use was restricted to women and the holes took about a year to fill. Then more holes were dug.®

In 1934/1935 the Rockefeller Foundation promoted bored hole latrines in Myanmar, Malaysia, Sri Lanka and Indonesia. The usual practice was for the local government or planters' association to provide an auger on loan. The boreholes usually went down to the groundwater table.®

The soil in the Nile Delta is particularly suitable for boreholes. In the late 1940s many were dug about six metres deep and 400mm diameter. There was no trouble with fly breeding.®

Slabs for borehole latrines can be quite small (sometimes only 300mm square) and so may be picked up and moved when a new hole is bored.

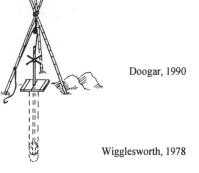

Doogar, 1990

Wigglesworth, 1978

Weir *et al*, 1952

Raised pits

Where hard rock or groundwater near the surface prevents the excavation of deep pits the volume available for accumulation of solids can be increased by building raised pits. The latrine floor slab is built above ground level and the pit lining is extended up to the slab. On steeply sloping ground part of the pit may be below ground level, and part above, as in the pit shown here in Freetown.

A brick or block lining that is above the ground should be made impervious above and immediately below the ground level. This may be done by cement rendering inside and outside. The watertight lining usually extends about half a metre below ground level.

Access to a raised latrine is usually gained by steps and the latrine is called a 'step latrine'. It is sometimes suggested that people do not like step latrines because they are 'exposed' when going up or down the steps. However, this is not always so. I have taken several photographs of men, women and children on the steps of these latrines. Alternatively excavated soil is heaped round the lining above ground level and the latrine is then a 'mound latrine'.

In Myanmar where old oil drums were used as pit linings, raised pits were built about a metre above ground level at the start of the monsoon season. An earth bank was raised around the lining.®

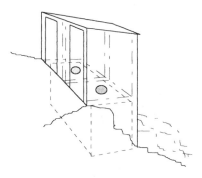

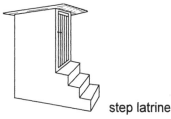

step latrine

Wilson, 1978

MacAuslan, 1985.

Hardoy et al, 1992

Baskaran, 1962

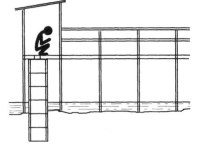

Pits in swamps

Many squatters live on land that is permanently or seasonally flooded or marshy. For example, in 1975 it was estimated that 60 per cent of the population of Guayaquil in Ecuador were in shanty towns above mud and polluted water, living in huts perched on poles.® Some houses are a forty minute walk from dry land. Large settlements of poor people live on land prone to flooding and tidal inundation or under water in Recife, Monrovia, Lagos, Port Harcourt, Port Moresby, Delhi, Jakarta, Buenos Aires, Resistencia and many other places.® Satisfactory sanitation always presents special problems for these people.

One method of construction in flooded areas is to lower concrete rings and build them up one on top of the other to the floor of the latrine. The storage capacity can sometimes be increased by digging out mud inside the bottom rings.

In the 1950s a number of pit latrines were built in a marshy, water-logged area in Kerala.® During the monsoon a part of the area is under water. Various linings were tested and it was concluded that pit latrines can be used in water-logged areas provided linings of concrete or soil-cement blocks are used.

Often the water over which these squatters live is highly polluted. In some places where groundwater is not polluted and it needs to be protected, pollution can be reduced by giving pit a 500mm thick 'envelope' of fine sand.

Summing up

This Chapter is the longest in the book because pit latrines are the most common form of low cost sanitation. Many variations are in use. All are reasonably simple so that householders can often build their own. The greatest disadvantage is the danger of groundwater pollution, which is discussed in Chapter 7. This danger is often over emphasized.

Chapter 5: EXCRETA AS A RESOURCE

a. The value of excreta

SINCE ANCIENT TIMES manure from farmyard animals has
been used as a fertilizer and soil conditioner. 'Muck spreading'
was once part of rural workers' routine work in Europe. For
various reasons during this century animal manure has largely
been replaced by artificial or chemical fertilizers which consist
of carefully measured quantities of nitrates, phosphates and
other material required by plants for growth.

Human or animal excreta contains nutrients like those in
artificial fertilizers. In many ways excreta is better than
chemicals. Artificial fertilizers do not contain all the trace
elements required by plants, but they are present in excreta.
Application of excreta encourages the formation of humus
which is essential for optimum soil structure and water
retention. Excreta promotes microbial life and the conversion of
minerals to biologically active forms. Experimental work in
India sixty years ago showed that adding a composted mixture
of vegetable waste and excreta enhances plant growth.® Plants
to which nightsoil compost is applied have been shown to be
resistant to diseases and the pests that cause them.

Howard & Wad, 1931

The Chinese have been able to farm the same fields for
over three thousand years because fertility has been maintained
by spreading their own excreta. In the middle of the 16th
century a visitor to China noted that 'the excrements of man are
good merchandise throughout China'. Now 90 per cent of
nightsoil is collected for agriculture® and there is a general
desire to use all human excreta as fertilizer.® In Shanghai three
millions tonnes of excreta are reused every year.®

Enfo News, 1989
Reed, 1994
Edwards, 1992

There are health hazards in spreading excreta in fields, but
appropriate methods of treatment and disposal can secure both
health and environmental benefits. Composting is a suitable
method of treatment.

The table on the next page® lists excreta use practices and
the sections of this book where they are described.

adapted from Cross, 1985

Practice	Social unit	Examples	Section of this book
Soil fertilization with untreated or stored nightsoil	family or community	China, Japan, Korea, Taiwan, Thailand	**7e**
Nightsoil collected and composted for use in agriculture	community or local authority	China, India	**6a**
Nightsoil fed to animals	family	China, India, Melanesia, Nigeria, Sri Lanka	**5e**
Use of compost latrines	family	Central America, Vietnam,	**5b**
Biogas production	family or community	China, India, Korea	**5d**
Fishpond fertilization with treated or untreated nightsoil	family or community	China, India, Korea, Malaysia, Indonesia	**5c**
Fish farming in stabilization ponds	Family (illegal) or local authority	India, Israel	**5c/7c**
Aquatic weed production in ponds	family, community or local authority	Vietnam, SE Asia	**5c**
Agricultural application of sewage	local authority or commercial farmer	India, Mexico, South Africa	**7c**
Irrigation with stabilization pond effluent	local authority or commercial farmer	India, Israel	**7c**
Algae production in stabilization ponds	local authority	Japan, Mexico	**5c/7c**

The value of urine

Stored urine quickly breaks down to ammonia which is toxic to plants and animals. However, when diluted with twice or more its volume of water and applied to soil the toxin is quickly neutralized and the nutrients absorbed. Ammonia in urine was used in Europe during the 19th Century for household cleaning, softening wool, hardening steel, tanning leather and dying cloth. In northern Nigeria indigo plants are still fermented in vats of urine to produce the irridescent blue that is a feature of local cloth.®

BBC, 1994

In the 1970s Chinese scientists found that amino acids in urine can be profitably extracted for the pharmaceutical industry. Shanghai's Bureau of Environmental Sanitation collects 200 tonnes of urine a day from public latrines and sells it to the Biochemical and Pharmaceutical Laboratory and other concerns. It is best used as a blood coagulant in surgery, and is exported to Europe, Japan and the United States.®

Robson, 1991

b. Compost latrines

When faeces decompose aerobically there may be a rise of temperature which destroys pathogens and thus a good land conditioner/fertilizer is formed. Required conditions include a suitable carbon to nitrogen (C/N) ratio, a low moisture content and access to air to ensure aerobic conditions, at least in the early stages of decomposition. These conditions are provided in compost latrines.® There are two types — continuous and batch — and some variations to details.

number of days in compost heap

Jeeyaseelen et al, 1987

Continuous compost latrines

Latrines of the 'Multrum' type use the continuous process. Excreta and vegetable waste are added to a receptacle, which is commonly made of fibreglass in Sweden, the United States and Canada. The mixture of excreta and vegetable matter slides down a sloping floor and is removed from a storage chamber. The material is kept aerobic by ducts and may remain in the receptacle for several years.

In Sweden a bed of peat moss, garden soil and grass clippings is spread on the floor of a new Multrum to ensure that the moisture content is not too high and to provide a good bacterial population for initial composting. For good operation about eight times as much vegetable waste as faeces is added to give a C:N ration of about 30.

Originally a Swedish design,® the Multrum has been strongly supported for environmental reasons in industrial countries. ® A version with an electric fan to keep air moving through the composting waste was claimed to be suitable for isolated beauty spots and beaches in the UK and other industrialized countries.®

Nimpuno, 1978

Stoner, 1977

Coghlan, 1993

Attempts have been made to introduce low-cost versions in developing countries.® However, experience in Argentina, Botswana, Dubai, the Philippines, Tanzania and other countries were not successful.® Compost units I inspected in Africa were the most unpleasant and foul-smelling household latrines I have experienced. The trouble was that the mixture of excreta and vegetable matter was too wet, and insufficient vegetable matter was added, especially during the dry season. Latrines used for bathing after defecation were especially bad.

Winblad et al, 1985

UNCHS, 1984

Double vault compost latrines

In the batch or double vault system, as introduced in Vietnam,® two watertight chambers are used alternately. A filler is added to provide carbon which lowers the C/N ratio. Without enough filler some of the nitrogen in compost latrines is lost, and the compost is less valuable as a fertilizer. Ash has been used as a filler in Vietnam and Central America. Elsewhere waste vegetable matter is added. Soybean leaves are reported to be especially good. Sawdust, cut-up waste paper and shredded leaves are also suitable as fillers.

Nimpuno, 1981

Besides providing a source of carbon, ash controls smells and helps to keep the mixture fairly dry. Urine is collected separately, diluted and itself used as a fertilizer. After a few months composted material is removed through small doors.

In Vietnam the latrines were earlier referred to as 'septic bins', the word 'bin' emphasizing the need to keep the contents dry.® For the same reason compost latrines are known as 'dry box latrines' in Central America, where thousands have been built since the late 1970s.®

McMichael, 1978

Winblad, 1994

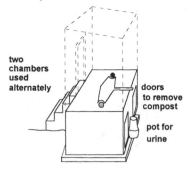

In Vietnam the floor of the bins was above ground level to exclude surface water. Before the bin was used a layer of ashes or lime was put at the bottom to absorb liquid and prevent faeces sticking to the floor. Smell was controlled if ashes weighing about a third of the weight of faeces were added. The temperature only rose a few degrees above the ambient temperature, but most helminths were reported to be killed in about eight weeks. When these latrines were built and used by everyone, there was up to 85 per cent reduction in diarrhoea and 50 per cent reduction in worms. When compost was applied to fields the crop yield increased by up to 70 per cent.

Because of pollution to Lake Atitlan in Guatemala the government attempted to introduce pit latrines. The people were not interested as they saw no benefit. In fact, as they were accustomed to easing themselves in the fields, their farms would lose fertilizer. Compost latrines were introduced in 1978 and immediately became popular.® Ash was added regularly, keeping the material dry and raising the pH. So they were named DAFF (dry alkaline fertilizer family). However, when the project was evaluated in the early 1990s only 23 per cent of households used the latrines properly.® Similar latrines were also built in neighbouring Honduras and Nicaragua.®

Hunt, 1986

Yacoob et al, 1992
Buren et al, 1984

In Guatemala farmers removed solids after about ten months. They were then sun-dried and stored in sacks until required on the land. In the cool highlands many roundworm eggs were still viable after a year, but sun-drying produced a hygienically safe product.® Dry box latrines have worked well in El Salvador. Sawdust and lime are added and the composted material is used to reclaim waste land or is put into bags and sold, the contents of a bag fetching the equivalent of US$ 10.®

Strauss & Blumenthal, 1990

Winblad, 1994

Other types of double chamber compost latrines have been developed in India and elsewhere. The Gopuri latrine devised at the Gopuri Ashram in Maharashtra is similar to the Vietnamese latrine, but has a vent pipe. Only a few have been built. In the Sopa Sandas latrine the chambers are offset, with inclined chutes from the squat hole, like the ROEC. Eighty thousand Sopa Sandas latrines were built in Maharashtra in the 1970s. Sheet metal flaps were fitted at the lower ends of the chutes to prevent flies escaping. However, in the corrosive atmosphere the flaps soon deteriorated. Hinges of similar flaps examined in Tanzania corroded so badly that the flaps fell off. There is no floor to the chambers of Sopa Sandas latrines, so excess liquid percolates into the soil.

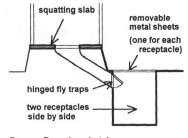

Sopa Sandas latrine

Compost latrines are most suitable where users are keen to operate the system carefully because they want compost for fields or gardens. Water and urine must be kept out and sufficient material with high carbon content must be added. Compost must remain in the bins long enough to avoid risk of disease transmission.

For an integrated rural health and development project near Dhaka, government policy promoted gooseneck pour-flush latrines that required two bucketfuls of water to clear. Water was scarce, plots were small and subject to flooding. So it was decided to try compost latrines that need no water, require less area and can be built above ground level. Sixteen latrines with small brick-built chambers were provided with bamboo and matting shelters. Urine was not collected but allowed to flow over the sides. These latrines were not liked. Users had to lean forward to urinate and wash their hands. People forgot to put ash in. The compost contained living helminth eggs. Construction costs more than pit latrines and so little compost was produced that it was not worth the trouble.®

Shafiuddin & Bachman, no date

Allowing water or urine to get into the chambers has been a major cause of unsatisfactory performance of compost latrines. In wet climates a roof is needed to keep out rainwater. Prohibition of the use of water is necessary. Consequently the system discourages hand-washing after defecation. Adequate cleaning of the latrine slab is virtually impossible without water ® although ash is sometimes used for cleaning.®

UNCHS, 1984
Jeeyaseelen et al, 1987

c. Aquaculture

Aquaculture is farming in water just as agriculture means 'farming on fields'. Carp and tilapia are especially good for fish culture. Ducks are cultivated on ponds. Crops grown in water include water spinach, water hyacinth, water chestnut and lotus.® Micro-algae are also cultured and harvested.

Mara & Cairncross, 1989

Faeces can provide nutrients for plant growth and hence for fish feeding on vegetation. In some places, particularly in Asia, raw sewage is discharged to fish ponds. Fish are also cultivated in ponds forming the final stage of some methods of sewage treatment. Collected nightsoil, sludge from pits, vaults or septic tanks or slurry from biogas units are sometimes deposited in fish ponds. Latrines are placed over ponds (*overhung* latrines — see page 76) or on the banks with pipes leading to the pond. Fish reared in ponds with overhung latrines were reported in China in the 19th Century® and the practice has existed since antiquity.

Turner, 1894

Calcutta's sewage is discharged to the 'wetlands' to the east of the city. These wetlands consist of 4500 hectares of ponds and form the largest wastewater-based aquaculture in the world. Indian carp, Chinese carp and tilapia are harvested. Between 1954 and 1984 six thousand tonnes of fish were caught there by about four thousand families. This is about 10% of the fish consumption of the metropolis.®

Furedy and Ghosh, 1984

In Bhopal young fish reared in waste stabilization ponds were longer and much heavier than similar fish reared in nursery ponds.® In Indonesia over thirty thousand tons of fish were harvested each year in about ten thousand hectares of ponds.®The bottom mud was removed from time to time and used as a soil conditioner and fertilizer on rice fields.

Bhatia & Sastry, 1982
Strauss & Blumenthal, 1990
Mara & Cairncross, 1989

In China the mean yield of fish in ponds is 3200 kilograms per hectare per year and up to seven tonnes are produced in some ponds. Although the traditional practice was to put fresh nightsoil into ponds, it is becoming usual to first store excreta in closed containers for a month or so.

Rather than direct feeding of excreta into fish ponds, fish may be grown in the last (maturation) ponds of a series of waste stabilization ponds.® The ponds must be kept aerobic and low ammonia levels maintained. Up to three tonnes of fish per hectare per year have been produced in maturation ponds.

Meadows, 1983

If fish fed on excreta are eaten by humans they should be properly cooked. Insufficient cooking may result in transmission of the oriental liver fluke and other pathogens.® Therefore fish fed with excreta are sometimes processed to form high protein meal for other fish or livestock.® Alternatively, algae or duckweed are harvested® and fed to cattle, poultry, pigs or fish, or composted to provide fertilizer.

Cairncross, 1988

Edwards, 1992
Polprasert et al, 1980

d. Biogas

Household biogas plants are widely used in China for treatment of human excreta in combination with animal and agricultural waste. Compared with the age-old system of open compost dumps, using watertight and gas-tight tanks produces a fertilizer that has a higher nitrogen and phosphorus content.® The gas is used for domestic cooking and also for powering vehicles, farm

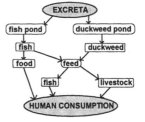

Buren, 1979

Gupta, 1983

Subramanium, 1978

Winblad et al, 1985
Remedios, 1981

machinery and electricity generators. The majority of pathogens are destroyed, although the removed slurry is not 'safe' as it contains upwards of one per cent of the helminth eggs in the feed.

Most Chinese biogas plants are built by the household or local community using local material. A common design has a domed roof. If it is later necessary to enter a tank for cleaning or repair, stringent precautions are necessary to avoid suffocation by poisonous gas. The main input is pigs' excreta.

In India biogas plants have floating domes which act as reservoirs for the gas. The dung from a family's cows is added. Sufficient gas for family lighting and cooking can be obtained in a 7-10 cubic metre plant fed with the excreta of a family of five and the dung of three or four cattle. In 1978-9 two communal biogas plants using cow dung were built in a small Indian village. After a good start, the scheme failed due to non-cooperation of villagers.®

Exceptionally, a few plants operate with human excreta alone. In a communal latrine at Gopeshwar, pour-flush latrines discharged directly into a circular chamber with a dome for collecting gas. Sulabh International has also included biogas production in some of their large public latrines. Nightsoil was collected from a thousand prisoners in the Central Prison at Nagpur.® Gas production was about twenty litres per person per day and was used in the prison kitchens.

e. Food for animals

Although reuse of excreta as animal food is not an important sanitation alternative, *pig latrines* justify brief mention. In China the practice of building a latrine over a pig pen was once common but is now discouraged.® There are examples in India ® and Nigeria and perhaps other countries. At Kalutara in Sri Lanka, I saw pigs wandering freely near a group of household pig latrines. Villagers whistled before relieving themselves and the pigs rushed to the latrines.

Transmission of disease is likely unless meat is properly cooked, but feeding animals with algae, duckweed and fish obtained by aquaculture reduces this danger.

Chapter 6: REMOVAL SYSTEMS, SEPTIC TANKS AND AQUA PRIVIES

SEWERAGE IS AN 'off site' method of dealing with excreta, as opposed to pit latrines, compost latrines and septic tanks where excreta is dealt with 'on site' or 'on plot' and only the sludge or dry solids may be removed and taken off site. Conventional sewerage is high cost, but some off-site systems are low cost. Low cost off site systems are rarely satisfactory, but are discussed briefly in this chapter. We also consider septic tanks and aqua-privies, which are on-site systems.

a. Container systems

The system of retaining excreta in a bucket or other receptacle was formerly very common and known as 'conservancy'. Removal is sometimes called 'nightsoil collection' because it is often carried out during the night. Nightsoil collection is being phased out in most countries where it is still practised. The system is condemned because the work is unpleasant and socially unacceptable, involving the collectors being exposed to disease. Nightsoil is often spilled, and there is fly and smell nuisance. Nevertheless, in the 1990s there are still many millions of households served by container systems, most of which are organized informally.

Until the 1960s there were many well-organized collection systems. Buckets under a seat or squatting slab were regularly removed through a small door at the rear of the latrine. In some places full buckets were taken to a depot and replaced by clean empty buckets. My own family had a bucket latrine at our house in West Africa in the 1950s. The 'conservancy man' called each night and emptied our full bucket into a larger container.

A variety of receptacles are used. Buckets and empty oil tins are common in Africa. In the Indian sub-continent baskets were usual. They were emptied from what were called 'dry latrines' by 'sweepers', many of whom were women. In 1992 I was told in Delhi that there were still

Whittington et al, 1992

about half a million dry latrines in that city alone.

In the early 1980s empty vehicle battery cases were commonly used in Karachi. They were fairly small, so soon overflowed. In Myanmar I saw wooden boxes used as containers. In 1994 I was shown several dozen bucket latrines in Freetown. Many of them were in police barracks.

A practice in some West African cities is for collectors to put nightsoil into holding tanks on sanitary sites, from which it is removed by vacuum tankers.® Bucket emptying is done by private contractors, most of whom empty the waste in local rubbish dumps or nearby streams close to the buildings from which the buckets are collected. Surprisingly, in 1990 two-thirds of users of household bucket latrines in Kumasi were satisfied with them, as they provided reasonable privacy and convenience.

Chemical toilets (or chemical closets)

Wright, 1960

These have containers in which a sterilizing liquid prevents nuisance from odour or flies. Portable buckets are widely used for building sites, open-air festivals and exhibitions. Over two hundred chemical closets were installed in Westminster Abbey for the coronation of Queen Elizabeth II.®

Chemical toilets in industrial countries usually have two containers, both commonly made of plastic or fibre glass. The outer container has a seat with a hinged cover. The inner bucket, which receives excreta, has a handle so that it can be lifted out of the outer container. Usually a measured quantity of a propriety liquid is diluted with water and put in the inner bucket to a depth of a few millimetres. When the bucket is nearly full the contents are tipped into a holding tank from which they are removed by a vacuum tanker. In isolated rural areas the contents are sometimes tipped into pits, although this practice may be prohibited by local regulations.

Containers are sometimes fitted beneath a toilet pan in aeroplanes, long-distance coaches and boats. When a switch is pressed, liquid is pumped from the container through a filter and is delivered as a flush to the toilet pan. The liquid usually drops into the container, but in some toilets the liquid is lifted from the pan by vacuum.

During servicing the container contents are discharged by gravity or vacuum to a tanker lorry or storage tank.

b. Vaults

Another removal system is the vault, a watertight chamber or tank under or close to a seat or squatting slab. Vaults may be periodically emptied by scoops or buckets and the excreta taken away in barrels, carts or tricycles, or they may be emptied by vacuum tankers.

Vaults were used in unsewered parts of Cairo before the Greater Cairo Sewerage scheme was built. Most of the vaults were within houses. The contents were ladled out, carried through the house and put into tanks mounted on donkey carts. Some tanks were legally emptied into the sewerage system; but the contents of most were dumped in canals or on vacant land. Some sludge was sold to farmers. Similar vaults are in use in other towns in Egypt.

Vault and tanker system

A mechanized form of conservancy known as the 'vault and vacuum truck' or 'vault and tanker' system is widely used in Japan and other countries of east Asia.® The vault is emptied by a vacuum truck every three weeks or so. In some cities the collected excreta is treated by advanced processes operated on modern chemical engineering principles.® Vault/tanker systems are suitable for urban areas where access by tankers is possible and trucks can be properly maintained.

Doubting the reliability of reports of this system for a modern industrialized country, I questioned the Director of Sanitary Engineering of Japan whom I met at a WHO meeting in Geneva.® He assured me that about a third of Japan's people use this system in the 1990s.®

Comparison of the vault and vacuum truck system with sewerage in urban areas of Korea® showed that the annual cost of a conventional sewerage system was more than five times greater than the existing vault system. Health benefits and the total pollution load to the environment are about the same if separate sullage treatment is installed and the vault emptying system is efficiently operated.

Waste holding tanks are commonly used in China.® These are vaults of various size depending on the number of users. Some are emptied by suction tankers, but in some parts of China the contents become frozen during the winter and have to be dug out.

Pradt, 1971

Strauss & Blumenthal, 1990

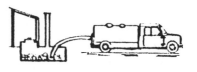

Magara, 1990
Kitawaki *et al*, 1994

Bradley & Raucher, 1988

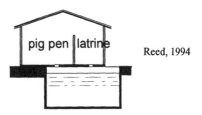

Reed, 1994

Chinese pig latrine

Cesspits

These are large watertight vaults for storage of sewage, usually from WCs in individual houses. The contents are removed by vacuum tankers periodically or when the cesspits are full. The need for regular emptying makes cesspits a very expensive form of sanitation.

Shahalam, 1986

About half the 7000 'septic tanks' in the city of Irbid in the north of Jordan were reported to have no soakaway in 1986.® They were, in effect, cesspits. With an average family size of twenty-one they were emptied on an average three times a month by privately-owned tanker lorries.

c. Overhung latrines

These are often built with a hole in the floor so that excreta falls into water underneath. They are particularly common in coastal areas and swamplands where dwellings are elevated on poles. There are many examples in Africa, Asia and Latin America.® In the Middle Ages a roofed four-holer latrine was built over the Thames at Temple Pier, south of London's Fleet Street.®

Egbuniwe, 1980

Reynolds, 1943

Lacey & Owusu, 1988

Residents of the congested settlement of West Point in Monrovia use makeshift latrines over the river or sea. Charges are made for the use of some of these.® In the bays along the coast at Freetown they are called 'wharf latrines'. Other overhung latrines are built over rivers, lakes and canals where the dwellings are on the banks.

Often water into which excreta falls is used for washing, drinking or other domestic purposes, either close to the latrine or downstream. There are then considerable health hazards. Bad smells and build up of solids often cause nuisance unless there is a strong current in the receiving water.In the development of the Gazira irrigation scheme in Sudan overhung latrines were built on bridges carefully located downstream of water intakes for the communities. Each scheme was fine on its own, but people drawing water further along the canal were forgotten.®

Sell, 1981

Overhung latrines are also used with algae tanks or fish ponds, briefly considered on page 70.

Unfortunately, there are few affordable sanitation alternatives for the many low-income communities whose homes are on stilts over water. One option may be a pit latrine with extended lining, described on page 64.

d. Conventional sewerage

Conventional sewerage consists of systems of pipes called 'sewers' that take waste water away from WCs, baths, kitchens and the like.® The system is also called 'waterborne sanitation' or 'watercarried sanitation'. The cost of conventional sewerage systems is very high, up to ten times that of on-site sanitation.® Consequently various lower-cost non-conventional sewerage alternatives have been introduced in some countries, as outlined on pages 79-81.

Pickford, 1988

Sinnatamby, 1990

The liquid flowing in sewers is known as 'sewage'. Sewage is carried in the sewers to a treatment works or through an outfall into a body of diluting water such as a river, lake or the open sea. Unless there is adequate treatment (such as is provided by a well-designed and well-maintained waste stabilization system) the receiving water will be polluted.

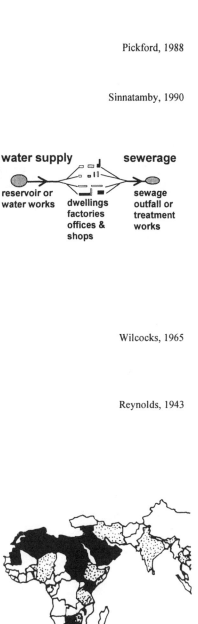

Some ancient civilizations boasted water-carried sewerage systems. At Mohenjodard in Pakistan an elaborate system of drains was built before 2000 BC. All houses had bathrooms and WCs which discharged through settlement tanks to brick-lined channels in the streets.® In India, Shah Jahan (1592-1666) loved the ladies of his harem at Agra so much that he built a toilet flushed with water perfumed with attar of roses. A similar latrine was built in the Amber Palace at Jaipur.® Flushed WCs connected to sewers only came into general use in Europe, North America and in some countries under the control of European powers towards the end of the last century.

Wilcocks, 1965

Reynolds, 1943

The high cost of sewerage is its greatest disadvantage. There is also the problem that it requires water for flushing. Most low-income people do not have piped water, and even those with water connections often have an intermittent supply. In many urban areas water is only available at low pressure for two or three hours a day. In several countries in Africa and Asia there is an overall and increasing shortage of water. This map shows in black the countries in which by 2025 there will be less than 500 cubic metres of water per person per year — too little for a modern country even with advanced technology. Countries marked with shading will have a serious seasonal shortage, with less than 1700 cubic metres per person per year.®

ENFO News, 1993

The syphon-operated WC cistern was invented and developed at Chelsea in London by Thomas Crapper in the nineteenth century. In recent times low volume cisterns and pans have been developed to reduce the amount of water used for flushing a WC, and hence to reduce the cost of sewerage. One type which has proved satisfactory in trials in Botswana and Lesotho uses a three to four litre flush.®

Swaffield & Wakelin, 1988

Advantages of sewerage

Provided design, construction and maintenance are good

- Sewerage is very convenient for the users, who have nothing more to do than keep the pan clean and operate the flush mechanism.
- Very low health risk.
- No nuisance from bad smells, flies or mosquitoes.
- Sullage (wastewater from bathing, washing and laundry) can be discharged to sewers.
- Sewers can take away industrial wastewater.

Disadvantages of conventional sewerage

- The cost is very high.
- The premises must be connected to an ample continuous reliable piped water supply.
- Construction difficulties are usual, especially in congested high-density areas.
- It is unsuitable for self-help - people cannot build their own conventional sewerage systems.
- Pumping is needed in flat areas.
- Maintenance is difficult.
- Concentration of pollution - see Section 7b.

Some difficulties with sewerage for low-income communities

- Blockage due to unsuitable anal cleaning material.
- Blockage due to other solid matter, such as ash and sand used for scouring pots and pans.
- Corrosion due to septicity at high temperature.
- Breakdown of pumping and treatment plant due to inadequate maintenance or power failure.
- Blockage due to low water use, or because few properties are connected to the system.

An example of low connection rates occurred in Accra, Ghana. A system with 29km of sewers serving an area of 512 hectares was commissioned in 1973. Three years later only 120 houses had been connected.®

Annan & Wright, 1976

Another problem (which does not occur often enough to be listed in the box above) is farmers stealing sewage for irrigation and fertilizer. This practice causes problems at Dhaka's pumping stations® and is reported in Lima.® I have seen above ground sewers broken by farmers in India and Nepal.

Mohammed, 1990
Strauss & Blumenthal, 1990

Two main systems — separate and combined — are common. In a separate system there are two sets of pipes. One takes the 'foul sewage' — the flow from WCs, domestic sullage and wastewater from commercial and industrial premises. The second set of pipes carries rain water away in 'storm sewers' or 'surface water sewers'. In a combined system all the sewage, both foul and storm, is taken by the same set of pipes.

separate sewerage system

combined sewerage system

In 1842 Sir Edwin Chadwick recommended the use of separate sewers in England. He used to say 'the water to the river and the sewage to the soil', because he believed in the value of excreta as a fertilizer. Yet in 1912 Allen Hazen, the eminent American engineer, argued that Pittsburgh should continue the combined system.® Generally the separate system is employed in the tropics because of high intensity of rainfall, which results in heavy runoff of surface water.

Kalbermatten, 1991

Sewerage is easier to construct and operate in places where the ground slopes. Sewers then follow the natural fall of the land and flow is 'by gravity'. In flat land, which is better for building cities, sewers gradually have to become deeper to give this necessary slope. After some distance sewers become so deep that excavation is excessive. Then the sewage has to be lifted by pumps of some kind, with increased costs and more trouble with operation and maintenance.

e. Non-conventional sewerage (NCS) or reduced cost sewerage

Because conventional sewerage is too expensive for most low-income communities, some saving in the capital cost has been achieved by one or more of the following.

- using smaller diameter pipes;
- laying pipes at flatter gradients;
- laying sewers at shallow depth;
- laying sewers within plots at the rear of premises;
- reducing the number and size of manholes; and/or
- providing interceptor tanks for settlement of solids.

Smaller than conventional size pipes laid at flatter than conventional gradients can be used where large solids are settled out of the sewage on or near household plots. Many NCS sewers have small interceptor tanks for each house. The tanks have to be emptied regularly, typically at six monthly intervals.

Experience of NCS systems

In some systems NCS sewers carry the effluent from septic tanks or aqua-privies. The 'aqua privy sewerage system'®, installed in several Zambian towns in the late 1950s and early 1960s, was a form of NCS. Four houses share a single latrine block built over a single tank, but each house has its own latrine and sink. Effluent from the tanks is discharged to small diameter sewers which lead to waste stabilization ponds..

Vincent et al, 1961

This diagram shows the layout of a typical NCS system in Brazil where sewers are shallow and are at the back of houses. This arrangement reduces the total length of the sewer and construction costs are comparatively low as the sewers are shallow. However, heavy vehicles have to be excluded if shallow sewers cross or run under roads. The system was criticized as a modification of an inappropriate system (conventional sewerage), retaining 'most of the disadvantages . . in addition to requiring a maintenance programme for the on site interceptor units'.® The system requires the co-operation of householders through whose plots the sewers run® and became popular as the 'condominial' system. In some places individual householders or neighbourhood groups are responsible for clearing blockages.

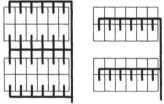

**conventional   shallow sewer
sewer layout   layout**

Greenhalgh, 1984

Sinnatamby *et al*, 1986;
    Reed & Vines, 1989;
    Vines & Reed, 1990

Khan, 1992

Pasha & McGarry, 1989

The NCS system in the *katchi abadi* of Orangi® in Karachi has been widely reported.® I have observed the gradual growth of the Orangi system during many visits to Karachi since 1979, most recently in 1993. There is now a network of low-cost sewers serving a large proportion of the million or so inhabitants. Some were built by the people themselves; some by contractors. The local communities, organized in 'lanes', have been responsible for all construction. The success of the Orangi Pilot Project (OPP) owes much to outstanding leadership, and has been assisted by suitable topography, widely available low cost building materials, a planned and regular site layout and a strong community desire to obtain sewerage through self-help.

Orangi sewage was discharged untreated into open drains and nullahs. NCS without treatment contaminates surface water, allows animals and flies to have contact with excreta and makes the environment of people living near the outlets malodorous, unsightly and unhealthy. So some people claim that greater benefits are obtained by on-site sanitation. Others argue that worthwhile benefits are achieved, even if treatment is not provided initially. This view was held by nineteenth century advocates of sewerage in the UK, who claimed that if human life was the prime consideration, the chief necessity was to move excreta from the immediate vicinity of people's homes 'even if it were at the expense of the purity of the rivers'.® To get this in perspective it is worth noting that in Latin America only two per cent of sewage is treated.®

Rawlinson, 1871

World Bank, 1992

A small NCS system 50 km south of Cairo served communal latrines at the school, mosque and guest house and all the 141 houses in the village. It was reported that the people liked the scheme, in which all the toilets were pour-flush.®

WHO-EMRO, 1992

In the State of South Australia, interceptor NCS systems are accepted as a proven and reliable technology. Between 1962 and 1986 over 80 small towns were served by such systems and new schemes were continually constructed. Systems were reported to be operating well twenty five years after they had been installed®. Only a few blockages occurred, and these were due to tree root intrusions.® However, Australian NCS schemes were only viable because of considerable government subsidies.®

SAHC, 1986

Otis, 1983
EPA (Melbourne), 1979

Vacuum systems

Pipe networks in which excreta is transported by air instead of water have been installed in some industrial countries.® Operation and maintenance are difficult as the whole system has to be kept air-tight.

USEPA, 1991

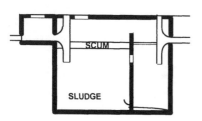

section through a
two-chamber septic tank

Septic tank

Soakpit

f. Conventional septic tanks

Septic tanks are watertight chambers that receive sewage from drains or sewers, usually from a single building or a group of nearby buildings. Grease and other light solids form a scum which in time may become quite hard. About two-thirds of the heavier suspended solids in the sewage settle and decompose anaerobically, giving off methane and other gases and leaving a residual sludge. The sludge has to be removed from time to time, as discussed below.

The liquid in a full septic tank (after settlement of sludge, flotation of scum and partial treatment in the tank) passes out of the tank as an effluent. Over time the effluent has the same volume as the sewage that enters, but the rate of flow is 'attenuated'. When a WC is flushed or a bath or sink is emptied the sewage enters the tank as a surge but leaves it slowly as a trickle.

Even though scum and sludge have been removed, the effluent carries a high load of microorganisms, which may include pathogens. It is also 'septic' because it has no dissolved oxygen. The effluent usually soaks into the ground from a soakpit or drainage field, as discussed in Chapter 7.

Advantages of septic tanks

> Well designed, constructed, operated and maintained septic tanks have the same advantages as sewerage, except that septic tanks do not usually deal with wastewater from industry.

Disadvantages of septic tanks

> - Very high cost.
> - They have the same water requirements as sewerage.
> - Sludge must be removed periodically to reduce blocking of soakage pits or drain fields.
> - There may be pollution of groundwater.

Design size of septic tanks

The capacity of a septic tank is the combined volume of the sludge, scum and liquid. Many formulae have been developed for the capacity. The British Code of Practice allows two cubic metres for accumulated solids and space for one day's flow of liquid, assumed to be 180 lpd.® A minimum depth of 1200mm is recommended for tanks serving up to ten people and 1500mm for more people. A formula devised in 1980® calculates the capacity required for the combined sludge, scum and liquid, and allows for variations of temperature, rate of inflow and method of anal cleaning. Another 'rational design'® allows for sludge accumulation at 40 lpy (litres per person per year) to occupy two thirds of the total tank volume.

Septic tanks may have more than one chamber. Most of the sludge is settled in the first chamber of a two-chamber tank. Liquid passes slowly to the second chamber so conditions there are less disturbed and more sludge is settled. Good design for a two-chamber tank gives the length of the first chamber as twice its width. The second chamber is square in plan. The opening between chambers should be below the scum and above the sludge in the first chamber. Some old-fashioned tanks have baffles extending from above the liquid surface to near the bottom of the tank. This is bad design as liquid passing under the baffle scours any sludge that has settled.

For small tanks inlets and outlets are best made with T-pipes. Larger tanks may have a baffle at inlet and a wier overflow at outlet. Other details of design have been published.®

Desludging

Septic tank sludge has to be removed from time to time. In some places de-sludging is carried out regularly every six months. Elsewhere tanks are desludged when the sludge occupies two-thirds of the capacity. Generally desludging is by vacuum tankers, although manual desludging is widely reported. About half of the replies to the WEDC postal survey® reported that some or all of the tanks in their districts wer desludged manually. The practice inevitably involves health hazards.

The accumulation of sludge was measured in a household septic tank in Kota Kinabalu after receiving the wastewater from a WC for five years. The rate of accumulation of sludge was 21 lpy.® The 1989 sanitation survey in Kumasi found that 40 per cent of septic tanks had never been emptied. The average time between desludging was ten months for the 60 per cent that were emptied.®

BSI, 1983

Pickford, 1980

Mara & Sinnatamby, 1986

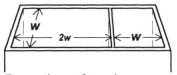

Proportions of good two-chamber tank

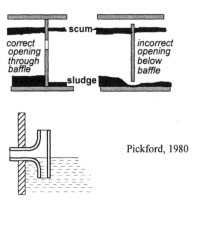

Pickford, 1980

Pickford, 1994

Bradley, 1983

The sludge is difficult to settle, consolidate or digest anaerobically. Aerobic digestion for a few days improves the dewatering characteristics.® In warm climates the development of anaerobic wastewater treatment may offer a viable alternative to conventional septic tanks. Experimental household units have been successfully operated in Bandung.® Sludge removal is only required every three or four years. The sludge from anaerobic reactors dewaters more easily than septic tank sludge. Treatment and disposal of septic tank sludge is discussed in Section i.

g. Small and extended septic tanks

A small tank and soakpit for WC waste only is used in many places. Sullage goes to roadside drains or separate sullage soakpits. There are obvious cost benefits over the conventional septic tank and soakaway that takes all wastewater. The small tank system is particularly suitable for small plots. Health benefits are claimed too.®

The performance of three small septic tanks in India was examined.® As they served pour-flush latrines, the flow was only between 5.4 and 6 litres per person per day. Sludge accumulation rates were between 25.8 and 36.8 litres per person per year. Comparing the influent and effluent, about 70 per cent of solids, 80 per cent of volatile solids and 93 per cent of 5-day BOD (biochemical oxygen demand) were removed. However, the effluent carried a fairly high load of live roundworm and hookworm eggs.

Jal Nigam, the water department of Uttar Pradesh, developed a dwarf (Bauna) septic tank from which sludge is removed every few weeks under hydraulic head and dried in a second open-bottom chamber. Effluent passes directly or through an upflow filter to an open drain.® In 1992 in India I was told by an engineer who had examined these units that desludging is difficult and that sludge is wet and pathogenic.

Some septic tanks that receive flow from pour-flush latrines are made of concrete pipes 750mm to 1000mm in diameter and 1.5-2 metres deep. The first chamber may have a layer of concrete at the bottom, but this is sometimes omitted on the assumption that the base will seal itself. If the bottom is not sealed the unit is a form of pit latrine.

Jewell *et al*, 1975

Lettinga *et al*, 1993

Bradley, 1983

Majumdar et al, 1960;
Bhaskaran, 1962

Sagar, 1983

Three-chamber septic tanks have been widely used in China and are reported in Vietnam.® A study in East Malaysia® considered a three-chamber system where WC flow goes to the first chamber and sullage to the second. The benefit is that the effluent is weaker than from a two chamber tank. So higher infiltration rates can be used for the soakaway or drainfield design. The three-chamber system saves space and enables septic tanks to be used at population densities up to 450 persons per hectare with an average wastewater flow of 120 lpd (litres per person per day) and an infiltration rate for the improved effluent of 30 litres per day per square metre.

UNCHS, 1984

Bradley, 1983

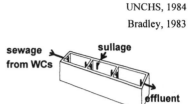

h. Aqua privies

An aqua privy is a small septic tank set beneath the latrine, with a pipe from the squat hole or pan to below the liquid surface. Overflowing liquid infiltrates to the soil from a soakpit or drainage field. The water level is maintained by adding a small amount of water, such as that used for cleaning the latrine. Sometimes sullage is added. Aqua privies were built in many countries between the 1940s and 1970s, but difficulties were often experienced in maintaining the water level because of leaking tanks. Daily maintenance is required with thorough cleaning of the chute to remove faecal matter adhering to the inner surface. If the tank is not regularly desludged, blockages occur and the latrine rapidly becomes a nuisance.®

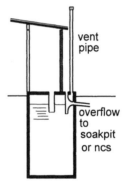

Peel, 1967

Many aqua privies were installed in the West Indies in the 1940s. A common type consisted of a precast concrete chamber with a precast concrete riser to form a seat.® In St Lucia a high density polyethylene unit proved popular. It was easy to keep clean and incorporated a shallow water seal which avoided trouble from smell and insects. Introduction of latrines of this type made a useful contribution to the control of bilharzia.®

Langshaw, 1952

Locally-manufactured GRP aqua privies were used for Khmer refugees in Thailand in the early 1980s. Most units had four pour-flush seats and two urinals, although a few were smaller. The aqua privy tanks overflowed to soakpits. Due to impermeable soil the soakpits were emptied by vacuum tanker following requests from leaders of community units. Desludging was carried out at intervals of

Unrau, 1978

Glensvig & Glensvig, 1989

Biellik & Henderson, 1984

Mishra, 1981

Maitra, 1978

Iwugo et al, 1978b

UNCHS, 1984

four to seven months.® There were considerable corrosion problems with the covers and superstructures. The units were expensive and were not considered suitable for long-term use.®

In the 1970s a voluntary agency, Maharashtra Gandhi Smarak Nidhi (MGSN) in Pune, popularized an aqua privy with a curved drop pipe.® This had the advantage that the water could not be seen while defecating, but inevitably resulted in more fouling of the pipe.

An ingenious design of aqua privy was introduced in Calcutta in the 1970s.® Both chamber and shelter were formed of pre-cast concrete panels and were hexagonal in plan. Excreta passed to the chamber through a water seal. However, the units cost considerably more than twin pit pour-flush latrines by which they were superseded.

Aqua privies, like septic tanks, require regular desludging. In 1978 I looked at several tanks under latrines built for the Zambian aqua privy sewerage systems twenty years earlier (see page 80). Many of the tanks were completely filled with solids. However, one of the advantages of aqua privies was claimed to be the ease of upgrading if conventional sewerage is installed nearby.®

Many communal *septic tank latrines* and *comfort stations* in West Africa and elsewhere have a tank beneath the floor. They are discussed in Section 9d. Household aqua privies with a 'drop-pipe' to below the water level went out of favour in the 1980s. There were two major problems — keeping the drop-pipe clean and maintaining the water level. In hot climates, five to ten litres of water a day are necessary to maintain the water level in a watertight tank.® With local workmanship it was often found difficult to make tanks that remained watertight, especially if the chamber was built with bricks or blockwork.

However, there have been many latrines built before and since which use the same idea. Decomposition of solids is assisted by keeping them wet in a watertight chamber whose overflow infiltrates into the soil from a soakpit. The VIP latrine and soakaway mentioned on page 48 and the public aqua privy latrine shown on page 129 are examples.

Chapter 7: TREATMENT AND DISPOSAL OF LIQUIDS AND SOLIDS

a. Disposal of liquids

LIQUIDS SOAK INTO the ground in all methods involving *infiltration* listed on page 36. These liquids consist of:

- urine;
- liquid from the decomposition of faeces;
- any water used for anal cleaning;
- water used to clean the toilet;
- water used to flush solids from a pan or along a pipe;
- rainwater if the shelter has no roof; and
- sometimes sullage (dirty water from washing, laundry, preparing vegetables,etc).

The quantity of liquid to be infiltrated may be taken as the following *litres per person per day* (lpd).

Pit latrine	
solid material used for anal cleaning	1.5 lpd
water used for anal cleaning	6 lpd
pour-flush latrine	10 lpd
Pit or drainfield taking sewage (eg from a septic tank)	
water from communal well or handpump	10 lpd
water from household well or yard tap	30 - 50 lpd
multiple-tap connection to water supply	50 - 300 lpd

A drainfield consists of trenches filled with gravel or broken bricks. It acts like a pit that is very long, but fairly narrow and shallow. Infiltration from pits and drainfields is mainly through the side walls. Some liquid goes through the base of a new pit or drainfield, but an impervious mat soon forms there, reducing the rate of infiltration.

Liquid from latrine pits and septic tanks contains large numbers of microorganisms of faecal origin, which may include pathogens. It also has a content of nitrates and other salts. The quantity of liquid from latrine pits is less than from septic tanks but the concentration of microorganisms and salts is likely to be greater. There is therefore the possibility that groundwater under or near to pits and drainage fields will be polluted.

Groundwater pollution

Groundwater is the 'saturated zone' where the space between the soil particles is filled with water. Groundwater pollution is most serious when it affects the quality of drinking water drawn from wells and boreholes. Water in leaking pipes laid below the level of polluted groundwater may also be contaminated if the pressure drops and groundwater enters the pipes.

If you want to find out more about groundwater pollution, refer to the thorough review by Lewis, Foster and Draser.®

Lewis et al, 1982

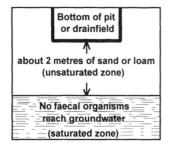

The two metre rule

> If there is two metres or so of fine sand or loam between the bottom of a pit or drainfield and the groundwater, virtually all bacteria, viruses and other faecal organisms are removed. In the soil above the groundwater there is little lateral movement of liquid. So water may be safely abstracted from a well or borehole a few metres away.

In 1920 it was found that bacteria penetrated 0.9 metres to 1.5 metres below pits that had been in use between one and three years.® In 1938 the vertical penetration of bacteria below a family pit was only 0.3 metres when the latrine was used normally.® Studies with septic tank effluent in the United States in the 1970s showed that bacterial pollution was less than two metres if the hydraulic loading was not more than 50mm per day® (that is 50 litres per day per square metre of the base area).

Klinger, 1921

Caldwell, 1938

Lewis et al, 1982

Of course this 'two metre rule' only applies where the groundwater level is lower than two metres below the bottom of the pit or drainfield *throughout the year*.

The horizontal movement of pollution is equally important. It has been suggested® that wells can safely be within eight metres of the pit or drainfield if the soil is fine. Fine soil is defined as having an effective size of 0.2 mm. In a two year long investigation of groundwater pollution in West Bengal over 5000 water samples were taken from 196 wells in fine soil around a pit latrine. Bacterial pollution travelled less than three metres horizontally, measurable 5-day BOD did not extend beyond 1.5 metres and at 4.5 metres chemical pollution became too dilute to be distinguished from groundwater.®

Wegelin-Schuringa, 1991

Baskaran, 1980

Sand envelopes

With coarse-grain soil (having an effective size larger than 0.2mm) it is sometimes recommended that the bottom of the pit should be sealed with impervious material such as a plastic sheet or puddled clay and the sides of the pit should be surrounded by 500mm of fine sand.® A 500mm envelope of sand adds considerably to the volume to be excavated and a great amount of sand is required. For example, if the pit is one metre in diameter the volume to be dug out would be increased four-fold. If the pit is three metres deep, seven cubic metres of sand weighing about eighteen tons would have to be brought in.

GOI/RWSG-SA, 1992

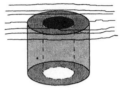

sand envelope around pit

Shallow groundwater

Where a pit or drainfield penetrates the groundwater, or is less than two metres above the groundwater, microorganisms travel with the groundwater. The 'safe' distance of a well from a pit or drainfield then depends on the velocity of the groundwater movement. Water becomes safe (free from living faecal organisms) after about ten days travel, so the safe distance is equal to the distance travelled by the groundwater in ten days. Heavy abstraction from a well or borehole increases the speed at which water moves and the risk of pollution is greater.

The velocity depends on the type of soil and the hydraulic gradient of the groundwater. Groundwater movement may be very rapid in cracked or fissured rock and pollution can go a long way from its source. On the other hand, living microorganisms may only reach a few metres in clayey silt. Recommended 'safe distances' such as 15 metres (often stipulated in guidelines and regulations) are reasonable for fine soil when it is not possible to estimate the groundwater velocity.

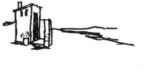

The National Environmental Engineering Research Institute (NEERI)® in India recommended that a pit should be *six* metres downstream of a water source such as a well. Instead of the two metre rule for vertical distance between the bottom of the pit and the groundwater table, NEERI recommends one metre. NEERI also points out that pollution does not travel so far when soil becomes clogged.

An extensive study of pollution of groundwater from pit latrines in Bangladesh was reported in 1987. A conclusion was that although hand operated shallow

Consortium, 1981

tubewells were contaminated by faecal pollutants, this cannot be correlated with pit latrines. The pollution was generally due to such factors as surface pollution, bad hygiene by users and faulty testing.

Where facilities for testing water are available the quality of the groundwater should be monitored. Particular attention should be given to bacteriological quality so that risk of pathogenic pollution can be assessed.

Chemical pollution

WHO, 1993b

Pollution by salts extends much further than pollution by microorganisms. Where there is high density of pit latrines or septic tanks the concentration of nitrates may build up to levels in excess of those recommended in WHO guidelines for drinking water.® There is then a fear that milk powder mixed with this water might lead to blue baby disease (methemoglobinemia) if given to very young infants. Breast feeding avoids this danger.

Amuzu, 1993

High nitrate concentrations have been reported in areas where there is no pollution from sanitation. For example in the largely rural Upper Region of Ghana concentrations up to 124mg/l in groundwater are reported. This is due to livestock wandering freely and the use of chemical fertilizers and animal manure.®

Pontius, 1993

Joint Committee, 1984;
   Forman, 1987

Dorsch et al, 1984

Evidence of other disease resulting from high nitrate levels is confused.® Some researchers have suggested that high nitrates may be associated with cancer, but stomach cancer was found to be *less* prevalent in areas whose water has a high nitrate content.®One study in Australia indicated that congenital malformation may be associated with mothers drinking water with high nitrate concentration during pregnancy.®

de Rooy, 1989

Industrialized countries pay a lot of attention to nitrate pollution because it results in algal growth in lakes and reservoirs. More serious for poor countries is the likelihood of diarrhoea and helminths when nitrate-rich but bacteriologically safe groundwater is rejected in favour of low-nitrate surface sources polluted with a variety of pathogenic organisms. In Kwara, Nigeria, five handpumps which gave bacteriologically safe water were closed because a chemist found too high nitrate concentrations.® The chemist should have compared the health hazards of the groundwater and alternative faecally polluted water.

Rise in groundwater

In some places overloading of soakpits causes a local rise in groundwater with resultant flooding. Flooding from soakpits occurred in Teheran.® Some soakpits in the more prosperous areas towards the north of the city were very large, receiving all household wastewater including WC discharges and sullage. In the 1970s I saw that the rise of groundwater from many such pits resulted in streams of wastewater flowing across lower level areas to the south. Children were playing in the wastewater which reached chest level of younger ones..

UNCHS, 1980

In Riyadh there was a similar problem that led to the 'rising groundwater' investigation in which WEDC was involved in 1988. Although water consumption was high, quite small soakpits had been provided for household septic tanks. The rise of polluted groundwater caused stagnant pools on vacant plots and even on roads near the soakpits.®

Pickford & Franceys, 1989

Disposal of liquids to surface waters

Regulations often prohibit the discharge to surface drains of effluent from septic tanks or overflow from pit latrines. From a public health point of view this is necessary because such liquids always contain a high concentration of faecal organisms. Children play in open drains and pools so the risk of spreading disease is high. Another environmental reason for stopping such discharges is the load of suspended solids that contributes to blockage of open drains. Blocked drains form stagnant pools, making ideal breeding places for Culex mosquitoes.

Sewage is often discharged to streams, rivers and lakes. Even with full conventional treatment, as discussed in Section 7c, effluent contains large numbers of faecal organisms and presents a health hazard to people who drink or use untreated water downstream. Only properly designed, constructed and maintained waste stabilization pond systems with adequate retention avoid this danger.

In 1948 the incidence of ascariasis (roundworms) amongst the Jewish population of Jerusalem dropped from 35 per cent to 1 per cent by cutting off the supply of wastewater for irrigation of fields producing vegetables. The use of raw sewage for agriculture was reintroduced in 1967 and within a year ascariasis in the residents of eastern Jerusalem increased to 60 per cent.®

Shuval *et al*, 1984

Effluent from septic tanks and aqua-privies

This effluent contains a high load of microorganisms of faecal origin and is therefore potentially pathogenic. The common practice of discharging effluent to open drains presents a severe health hazard. It is sometimes prohibited. For example, the Indian code® states 'under no circumstances should the effluent from a septic tank be allowed into an open channel or drain or body of water without adequate treatment'

Generally effluent is discharged to soakpits or drainfields for further treatment through the soil.

Soakpits are usually lined like pit latrines with materials such as masonry, bricks or concrete blocks. The volume is sometimes made equal to one day's flow. Alternatively the size may be calculated to give enough wall area for percolation, as described in Section 4a for latrine pits, allowing for the greater rate of percolation suitable for sullage.

Conventional household septic tanks may deal with all the wastewater, including sullage. Then a reasonably sized pit cannot normally cope with all the flow and drainfields are commonly used. Drainfields consist of trenches filled with stones or broken bricks. Drains with open joints or perforated pipes are laid in the trenches with a flat gradient. The length of trench should be enough for the walls below the pipes to give sufficient percolation area.

After soakpits or drainfields have been in use for some time, the pores of the soil around may become clogged. It then becomes necessary to dig new pits or trenches. Alternatively two trench systems may be constructed. When one is clogged it can be rested while the other is in use. Consequently a soakaway or drainfield should not occupy more than half the space available, leaving room for another if the first one gets blocked. If plots are too small, non-conventional sewerage should be considered for removal of septic tank effluent — see Section 6e.

Upward flow filters have been recommended for treatment of septic tank effluent. Filters built in West Bengal® produced a substantial reduction of BOD and suspended solids. De-sludging was carried out once or twice a year at the same time as the septic tanks were de-sludged.

Downflow/upflow filters have also been installed in

Indian Standards Institution, 1986

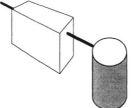

Raman & Chakladar, 1972

Africa where groundwater levels vary seasonally and the water is not abstracted for drinking. When the water table is low, the filter acts as a soakpit. In the rainy season effluent passes down one side of the filter, up the other side and then out to an open drain. This does not completely eliminate pollution, but is better than the common practice of discharging all effluent directly to drains.

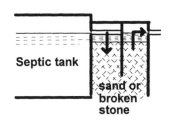

Septic tank

sand or broken stone

In industrial countries the effluent from large septic tanks is sometimes given conventional treatment, using small percolating filters or rotating biological contactors. Such treatment is occasionally provided for institutional septic tanks in developing countries.

Mound soakaways

These are sometimes used if the soil is unsuitable for a soakpit or drainfield because there is underlying hard rock, clay or high groundwater. The mound is built up of gravel and soil through which perforated or open-jointed pipes pass. Mounds only deal with about five litres of effluent per day per square metre, so need a lot of earth. Water goes to the atmosphere by evapotranspiration through vegetation planted on top of the mound. Alfalfa is a shrub which uses water at the fastest rate and is therefore suitable for planting on a mound. It is normally fed to animals.®

mound soakaway

Grace, 1986

b. Sewage treatment and disposal

When sewers were first built in Europe and North America sewage was normally treated by spreading on land. 'Water to the sea and sewage to the land' was the rule. Irrigation with sewage is still practised in several countries. In 1985 there were more than two hundred wastewater irrigation systems in India® and Mexico City had the largest wastewater reuse scheme in the world. Treated sewage is also reused for industry and exceptionally for public water supply. Muslim laws require an especially high standard of treatment.®

Mara & Cairncross, 1989

Farooq & Ansari, 1983

Irrigation with wastewater

Sewage from the city of Kanpur was mixed with equal volumes of diluting water and spread across over 1400 hectares. Wheat, paddy, maize, barley, potatoes, oats and vegetables are grown. Crop yields from land on which sewage is spread are much higher than those from land irrigated with clean water. In Pune papaya crops irrigated with wastewater were 1.38 times greater, potatoes 1.52 times greater, beetroot 1.86 times greater and okra over twice as great as crops on land irrigated by canal water with traditional manuring.

Irrigation with sewage entails risk of disease spreading, which varies with the type of crop. Farm workers are at risk with all crops. With crops grown for fodder, including pasture, those who consume meat are also at risk. With industrial products, such as sisal, risk extends to product handlers. Crops eaten raw present the greatest risks, especially plants near the soil (like lettuce) and root crops like radish and onions. The growing time of salad crops is often shorter than the survival time of pathogens So irrigation with sewage (or spreading untreated human excreta) is potentially harmful even when it takes place before planting.

Wastewater treatment

In industrial countries sewage farming has generally been replaced by treatment processes. The purpose of treatment is to reduce pollution to rivers, lakes or the sea to which effluent is discharged. Polluting matter which has a detrimental effect on receiving waters, especially inland waters, consists of the following.®

Oakley, 1983

Organic matter, which uses oxygen for decomposition and so takes oxygen from the receiving water. There is a *biochemical oxygen demand* (BOD). Provided the receiving water contains some dissolved oxygen decomposition of any organic matter takes place naturally. With heavy pollution, decomposition uses up oxygen more quickly than it is replaced, resulting in oxygen depletion, death of fish and other organisms, and production of unpleasant smells.

Suspended solids, which may be deposited on the bottom of receiving water, causing partial blockage of flow.

Pathogenic organisms, which create a danger of spread of water-carried disease.

Ammoniacal nitrogen, which can be toxic to aquatic organisms.

Toxic substances, usually arising from industrial wastewater.

Conventional sewage treatment

Conventional treatment involves separation of solids in sewage and then dealing with the solids and liquid separately. Methods of dealing with solids are generally those dealt with in Section 8d, as sewage sludge can be treated and disposed of in ways which are also used for solids removed from latrine pits, vaults and septics tanks. Separation of the solids is usually by screens (to remove rags, sticks and other large solids) and settlement of suspendfed solids (which produces sludge).

The main purpose of treatment of the liquid is to reduce the biological oxygen demand so that the effluent can be further treated naturally in the river or lake to which it is discharged. In sewage treatment, biological oxidation is basically a process to increase the rate of natural purification.

The two main methods are biological filters and the activated sludge process. Filters (also called 'percolating filters') normally consist of beds of hard material (called 'medium') such as gravel or broken bricks about two metres deep over which settled sewage is spread, usually from rotating pipes. Microorganisms which build up round the medium decompose organic matter. The process is aerobic because air circulates between the medium. For small flows an alternative to the filter bed is a 'rotating biological contactor'. This consists of a number of discs half submerged in liquid. Films of microorganisms form on the sides of the discs and are kept aerobic as the discs turn above the liquid.

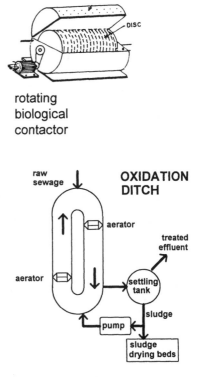

rotating
biological
contactor

In the activated sludge process, sludge is kept in suspension and is recycled. It is aerated by blowing air through or by mechanical agitation. A simple system is an oxidation ditch, where paddles aerate the liquid and move it round a channel shaped like a running track.

Following aerobic decomposition, sludge is settled and removed for treatment. Decomposition is not accompanied by extermination of microorganisms. Although effluents from conventional treatment plants contain few helminth eggs or protozoa cysts, they still have high concentrations of faecal bacteria and viruses, including pathogens. This results in serious health risks where the receiving waters are drunk without further treatment, as is common in most low income countries.

Waste stabilization ponds

Treatment in well designed and well operated waste stabilization ponds reduces pathogens. The long retention time - typically about twenty days - is enough for pathogens to die naturally in a hostile environment. Waste stabilization ponds have additional advantages of simplicity, the lack of mechanical equipment and incorporation of solids treatment in the ponds themselves. Their cost is lower than that for conventional sewage treatment, there is no (or very little) expenditure of energy, they can absorb shock loads and they can treat many industrial and agricultural wastes.® Maintenance largely consists of removing floating debris and keeping the edges of the ponds free from vegetation to discourage mosquito breeding. Ponds are therefore eminently suitable for developing countries. They are the first choice for wastewater treatment in warm climates wherever land is available at reasonable cost.®

Mara & Cairncross, 1989

Arthur, 1983

The oxygen concentration of wastewater in pond systems is increased by algal photosynthesis and wind across the surface. Ponds are shallow, typically one to one and a half metres deep, and to give sufficient retention time they require a large area of land. For strong sewage the first pond may be three or more metres deep and anaerobic. The area can also be reduced by installing aerators in the first pond. Aerated lagoons are deep ponds in which wastewater is aerated by rotating paddles. Installing aerators in a primary pond at Sana'a reduced the area required in the designed ponds by 60 per cent.®

Jackson, 1979

Irrigation with treated wastewater

Irrigation with treated wastewater has benefits for areas that are permanently or seasonally arid. These include increased agricultural production, improved food supply and reduced environmental pollution.® Most helminths can be removed by settling for two days. Ponds with twenty day retention eliminate almost all bacteria and viruses, producing an effluent that is suitable for unrestricted irrigation of vegetables, providing the sewage does not contain too much industrial effluent with high concentrations of heavy metals or toxic chemicals.

Shuval *et al*, 1986

Sewage effluent is increasingly considered as a valuable water resource, especially where rainfall is low.

However, groundwater may be polluted, especially if irrigated soil is underlaid with limestone or fissured rock. Also soil may be salinated, so attention should be given to drainage of irrigation water that has passed through the soil. This salty drainage water may be suitable for irrigation of salt-tolerant crops. Long-term damage to soil can be avoided by crop and field rotation.

In several middle eastern countries very high standards of treatment are required for effluent used for irrigation.® Tertiary treatment, sometimes followed by chlorination, is common, even where the reuse is restricted to municipal use (such as watering of roadside verges) or afforestation. Incidentally, chlorination of effluents is not a reliable means of eliminating pathogens unless there is a very high standard of operation control.® It is also very expensive.

Use of sewage effluent for irrigation provided a solution to the problem of groundwater depletion due to excessive abstraction of water in Gaza, occupied Israel.®

Cowan & Johnson, 1985

Mara & Cairncross, 1989

Abu-Hijleh, 1993

c. The problem of solids disposal

In many places it is difficult to dispose of nightsoil collected by the conservancy system and sludge removed from pit latrines and septic tanks. As cities expanded in 17th Century India the lack of suitable disposal grounds forced sweepers to dump collected excreta 'over the first waste ground encountered'.® Disposal of sewage sludge is also a problem at many modern sewage works worldwide.

Lowder, 1986

The material removed from septic tanks, known as *septage*, it is very much stronger than sewage or sewage sludge, as can be seen from this table.®

adapted from USEPA, 1984

Concentration mg/l	Design value for septage	US medium strength sewage	Ratio septage/ sewage
Total solids	40 000	720	55:1
Total volatile solids	25 000	365	68:1
Total suspended solids	15 000	220	68:1
5 day BOD	7000	220	32:1
COD	15 000	500	17:1
Alkalinity	1000	100	10:1

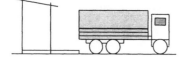

Mohanroa, 1973

Hawkins, 1981

Vacuum tankers normally remove the entire contents of septic tanks, except for some sludge that is left for 'seeding'. So septage consists of liquid, sludge and scum.

Nightsoil is rich in nutrients. In India in the early 1970s the average total solids was ten to twelve per cent. The solids contained 3-5 per cent nitrogen, 2.5-4 per cent phosphorus and 0.7-1.9 per cent potassium.® Pit latrine sludge is thicker. On average of the sludge from fifty pits in Botswana and Tanzania had 20 per cent sand and 25 per cent organics.®

d. Treatment and disposal of solids

Methods of treatment and disposal are similar for the contents of pit latrines and vaults, for nightsoil and for sludge. Alternative ways of dealing with all these sludges are therefore considered together in the table on the next pages.

Strauss, 1985

USEPA, 1984

Nightsoil, septage and pit/vault solids usually contain many living excreted organisms, which may include pathogens.® Septage has a concentration of organisms similar to that of raw primary sludge, as shown below.®

No per 100 ml	Total coliforms	Faecal coliforms	Faecal streptococci
Septage in Norway	3.5×10^7	3.9×10^6	4.7×10^3
Average USA septage	$10^7 - 10^9$	$10^6 - 10^8$	$10^6 - 10^7$
Raw primary sludge in Norway	5.6×10^7	2.0×10^7	1.1×10^6

The only untreated sludges that are free from living excreted organisms are those from properly-operated twin pit latrines, as described on page 55, where the solids in the 'resting' pits have been left for at least a year; or from dry box compost latrines (see page 68) with at least six months retention.

Treatment in waste stabilization ponds (Method 8 in the table) can also eliminate all pathogens provided the retention time is more than three weeks, there are at least three ponds in series and there is no short circuiting. Retention in sludge lagoons, like those at Freetown shown here, requires much longer to eliminate all pathogens.

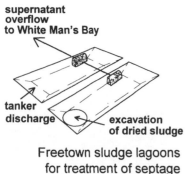

supernatant overflow to White Man's Bay

tanker discharge   **excavation of dried sludge**

Freetown sludge lagoons for treatment of septage and pit contents

Methods of dealing with septage, nightsoil and the contents of vaults and pit latrines

Method and brief description	Limitations	
1. Natural drying Spread in layers 200 - 300 mm thick on underdrained gravel beds; removed when dry and used as land-conditioner or landfill.	Some sludges do not dry naturally; some climates are too wet; dried sludge may contain helminth eggs.	Sewage sludge is often dried on open drying beds if sufficient area is available and there are suitable outlets for dried sludge. Septic tank sludge dewaters very slowly without pretreatment. [Jewell et al, 1975]
2. Trenching Put in trenches about a metre deep and covered with a 300 mm layer of soil; trenches redug after a year; material used as land-conditioner or landfill.	A large area of land is needed; fly-breeding may occur if cover is not deep enough; helminths may be transmitted if trenches are redug too quickly.	
3. Composting Mixed manually or mechanically with two to three times its volume of vegetable waste (e.g., selected municipal refuse); kept aerobic for several weeks, usually by turning; then matured in windrows; used as land-conditioner or fertilizer.	Often the cost of treatment exceeds the income from sale of compost, or compost cannot be sold; harmful material (e.g. glass, toxic waste) must be removed from municipal waste.	In the 1930s an emulsion of nightsoil and three times its volume of water was composted with street sweepings in Mysore. ® [Mieldazis, 1934] In co-composting of nightsoil from more than 60 000 people served by bucket latrines and refuse from 100 000 people in static piles with forced aeration at a township near Grahamstown, South Africa the temperature rose to over 50° and helminth eggs were destroyed.® [La Trobe & Ross, 1992]
4. Disposal on land a. Dumped on open land. b. Used as fertilizer without prior treatment.	a. Environmental damage and health risks. b. Common in East Asia; high health risks	Dumping on open spaces is probably the most common method of disposal of pit and septic tank contents worldwide. Spreading of septage on grass gave good uptake of nutrients; when later cut and stored there was no danger of spread of pathogens.® [Carlton-Smith & Coker, 1985]

Methods of dealing with sludges, nightsoil and the contents of vaults and pit latrines (continued)

Method and brief description	Limitations	
5. Disposal in water a. Dumped in rivers, canals or the sea. b. Treatment in ponds - aquaculture [see Section 5c].	a. Environmental damage and health risks. b. Requires marketing of algae, fish and/or ducks	In the early 1970s I often looked from the old Carter Bridge in Lagos at nightsoil being tipped into the lagoon below.® [Sridhar & Omishakin, 1985] Later aerated lagoons were constructed on the north of Lagos Island.® [Hindhaugh, 1973]
6. Biogas a. Added to household-size biogas units, whose main input is animal waste [see Section 5d]. b. Mixed with primary or secondary sludge at sewage works.	a. Ammonia content may inhibit biogas generation. b. Digesters must have capacity for increased load	The capacity of sludge digestion tanks at sewage works in Kuala Lumpur was increased to allow for septic tank sludge.® [Hogg & Dwyer, 1958].
7. To sewers Dropped down manholes or at specially-constructed discharge stations.	Satisfactory if there is good flow in the sewers and the treatment works can cope with increased load.	Tanks for vault contents from unsewered areas were included in designs for the Greater Cairo sewerage project.
8. To sewage treatment Added to sewage flow at sewage works.	Added to the inflow of waste stabilization ponds and conventional plants with primary sedimentation; added to surplus sludge for extended aeration.	Nightsoil was successfully treated in ponds in South Africa.® [Shaw, 1962] Solids are co-treated with sewage in ponds at Gaborone, Dar es Salaam, Amman and towns in Malawi.® [Strauss, 1993]
9. Special treatment Treated in plants specifically designed for septage, nightsoil or pit/vault contents.	Advanced treatment processes are used in Japan,® [Ikeda, 1972] Korea etc; stabilization ponds are suitable if sufficient dilution water is available.	A series of holding tanks in Accra deal with collected septic tank sludge and pit contents; solids in the effluent has strength equivalent to raw sewage. Settled solids are composted with sawdust. In Freetown septage and pit contents are treated in two lagoons shown on page 98, which are used alternately.

PART C
GETTING APPROPRIATE SANITATION

Chapter 8: INDIVIDUAL EFFORTS

a. Paying for latrines and willingness to pay

A WORLD BANK publication on hand pumps says that 'the technology should give the community the highest service level that it is willing to pay for, will benefit from, and has the institutional capacity to sustain'.® The same could be said of payment for latrines by householders.

Arlosoroff et al, 1987

When planning a latrine programme there is sometimes confusion between *affordability* and *willingness to pay*. It has often been said that people cannot afford more than five per cent of their income on water and sanitation — or two or three per cent on sanitation. So attempts are made to keep latrine costs low enough for the household contribution (with or without subsidy from an agency) at less than two or three per cent of the estimated average income of the community

However, there are many reports of people paying a great deal for water. In Onitsha, water cost slum-dwellers 18 per cent of the household income.® In Nouakchott, Mauritania, the price to vendors in 1981 was a hundred times that paid by those with piped water supplies.® Similarly, there may be willingness to pay highly for sanitation if it is really wanted.

World Bank, 1992

Theunyck & Dia, 1981

Paying highly for sanitation

In Tegucigalpa (Honduras), loans up to $300 per family repayable in three years were offered to the urban poor through the Co-operative Housing Foundation and UNICEF. Although interest rates were high (17 per cent per year) and the Ministry of Health had a long-standing policy of providing a free service, many people took up the option and built a sanitation unit with water tank, washboard, shower and latrine.®

Aasen & Macrae, 1992

Danida, 1991

Chadha & Strauss, 1991

Whittington et al, 1992

In a rural area of Sri Lanka, householders paid on average about 70 per cent of the average monthly income for latrines provided under a bilateral aid programme.® A survey in Bangladesh villages found that 74 per cent of householders were willing to pay for the cost of a slab and two lining rings, most of which were taken away in handcarts, rickshaws or bullock carts.®

In the Kumasi Sanitation Project in Ghana, householders who made a ten per cent down payment were provided with KVIP latrines. The balance with ten per cent interest charges was repaid over three years. Many householders paid extra to make the latrines better. In 1992 I looked at many of the latrines built by this project and was surprised at the number of householders who had paid for extras like white or coloured wall tiles, terrazzo floors and white tiles to the front and bench of seats.

In the 'willingness to pay' survey before the project started® the amount people were willing to pay was reported as affected by the following. Many of the points are obvious without a survey!

- Householders with more income would pay more;
- owners would pay more than tenants;
- those already paying a good deal for sanitation would pay more;
- those most dissatisfied with their existing sanitation would pay more;
- willingness to pay was not influenced by educational level, nor by sociological and cultural variations.

For an improved service 88 per cent of respondents were willing to pay more than their present expenditure on sanitation.

Difficulties often arise where householders do not own their dwellings, as in most multi-occupancy buildings. Reasonably enough, owners generally will not pay for improved sanitation unless they can increase the rent, and tenants are generally unwilling to pay any lump sum for improvements to property which is not their own. The right to land (tenure) critically affects people's willingness to pay for sanitation. In Lima householders with tenure were on average willing to pay nine times as much on their dwelling as were those who had no land rights.®

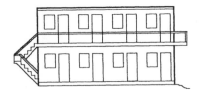

Soto, 1989

An example of very keen willingness to pay was reported from Zimbabwe, where Maika, a recently married community activist, built a VIP latrine in time for the first visit of his mother-in-law to the new home. On arrival she said she could not use the same latrine as her son-in-law. Maika volunteered not to use it, but did not satisfy the mother-in-law as he had already used it. So Maika built a second VIP.®

Moyo, 1992

b. Costs (construction, operation and maintenance)

Overall costs

has been claimed that the investment cost of conventional urban sewerage is typically five times the cost of labour and materials. This increases by thirty to forty per cent when foreign loans are involved and by over 200 per cent when international tenders are required under loan agreements.®

Hasan, 1992

Where appropriate low cost sanitation schemes are managed by the local community or individual householders, costs may be limited to material and labour. Even so, supplies that have to be imported from abroad may have a range of prices from a low 'official' rate to many times as much in the open market. In Myanmar in 1991 the cost of cement in the open market was sometimes up to twenty times the official rate. Similarly, official conversion rates between local and hard currency may be entirely unrealistic.

In rural areas the economic value of labour may vary greatly in different seasons. At some times everybody is busy in the fields and labour costs are high. At other times people are willing to work for low wages because they have nothing else to do.

Consequently, attempts to give international costs of different types of sanitation are usually of little value, even when they are expressed in a common currency, like the US dollar. Costs are also 'date-specific', so for comparison of figures obtained over the years a common date should be specified. Rates of inflation vary a great deal with time and also between different countries during the same period (see column b in Annex I).

Even allowing for economic juggling, the costs of similar services show great variation. For example, the

Feachem, Guy et al, 1983

Chadha & Strauss, 1991

Paramasivan, 1993

Davis *et al*, 1993

Samanta, 1993

annual cost in US dollars of providing a bucket latrine service in Kumasi in 1978 was four and a quarter times as much as in Ibadan, Nigeria, in the same year.® An alternative way of comparing costs is to give them in days or hours of labour and quantities of materials.

Costs of producing components may vary too. In 1990 it cost private manufacturers in Bangladesh more to make latrine slabs than it cost the Department of Public Health Engineering (DPHE), but concrete lining rings were cheaper made by the private sector than the DPHE.®

Use of different materials obviously results in different costs. For example in 1993 for the more-or-less standard twin pit pour-flush latrine in India the government and agencies like UNICEF paid householders 2400 rupees. In a village near Mysore latrines with the same design were built for 750 rupees. The saving was due to lining pits with stone obtained during well-digging and using lime mixed with a little cement for mortar in the shelter.® A similar case is reported from the village of Zezencho in Ethiopia. Model pit latrines with concrete slabs cost US$40, which the people could not afford. An affordable construction using local materials was adopted. For $12 a slab could be made with cedar logs and bamboo poles tied together with eucalyptus rope plastered with clay.®

In Medipur in West Bengal ten alternatives were offered at prices ranging from $10 to $100.® All were pour-flush pit latrines as shown below. Apart from offering alternatives to householders, this scheme enables latrine owners to upgrade their latrines as they have more money.

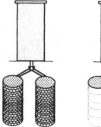
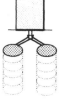
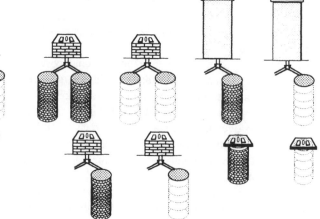

brick lining   **concrete rings**

Cost of sanitation alternatives

Comparison of the cost of conventional septic tanks and sewerage for houses that already had internal piped water supply in Malaysia showed that septic tanks are cheaper unless the population density was more than 150 to 180 persons per hectare. If a septic tank and soakaway only dealt with WC wastes (sullage going to roadside drains), sewerage only became cost-effective when population density exceeded 350 persons per hectare.®

In Nigeria in 1973 it was estimated that aqua-privy latrines cost twice as much as pit latrines, but only half as much as septic tanks.® In Kenya in the mid 1970s costs of various forms of sanitation compared with a simple pit latrine were estimated to be as follows.®

Bradley, 1983

Oluwande, 1978

Holland, 1977

Method	Capital cost	Life of unit (years)	Running costs
Pit latrine	1	8	1
Bucket latrine	0.27	0.5	4.75
Aqua privy: tank	5.3	15	2.7
soakpit	3	5	
Cesspit	40	20	24
Septic tank: tank	27	20	0.67
soakage	5	5	
Sewerage: sewers	13	40	0.67
conventional treatment	13	25	2.5
Sewerage: sewers	13	40	0.67
pond treatment	4	30	0.5

Comparisons of alternative systems in Botswana in the late 1970s® gave the following.

Bellard, 1981

    ROEC (see Section 4h) 1.59 times the cost of a VIP
    Double pit latrine   1.59 times the cost of a VIP
    Aqua-privy   2.46 times the cost of a VIP

A few latrines of various types were built in rehabilitation camps for refugees in Bangladesh. Costs compared with a simple pit lined with concrete rings and with a bamboo floor were as follows.®

Williams, no date

    Simple pit latrine   1.00
    VIP latrine   1.28
    water-seal latrine   1.39
    2-family aqua-privy   1.48
    5-family aqua-privy   1.61
    double vault compost latrine 3.14

Total annual cost per household (TACH)

A very useful figure for comparing sanitation costs is the *total annual cost per household* (TACH). This includes capital (or investment) costs and recurrent costs adjusted to reflect real opportunity costs averaged over time. 'Opportunity costs' are based on what money would buy now if not put aside to pay for future recurrent costs.

A World Bank study in 1978 found the proportion of the TACH to be as follows.®

Kalbermatten et al, 1982

	Technology	*Capital*	*Recurrent*
Low cost	Pour flush single pit latrine	71	29
	Pit latrine	100	negligible
	Communal septic tank	71	29
	Low-cost septic tank	79	21
	Compost latrine	92	8
	Bucket latrine	57	43
Medium cost	Sewered aqua-privy	78	22
	Aqua-privy	96	4
	Vacuum truck cartage	68	32
High cost	Conventional septic tank	62	38
	Conventional sewerage	67	33

The 1978 World Bank study also presented the total annual household cost for various types of sanitation as a percentage of the income of an average low-income household, as follows.

Low cost technology	Pour flush single pit latrine	2
	Pit latrine	3
	Communal septic tank	9
	Low-cost septic tank	6
	Compost latrine	10
	Bucket latrine	6
Medium cost technology	Sewered aqua-privy	11
	Aqua-privy	16
	Vacuum truck cartage	15
High cost technology	Conventional septic tank	29
	Conventional sewerage	26

These figures have been quoted extensively, largely because no other comprehensive data are available. However, their value is limited because of the following.

- They were based on a very limited number of examples in very few countries;

- since 1978 the costs of many materials (especially imported items) have increased relative to personal incomes in developing countries;
- interest rates have generally been much higher than the 8 per cent assumed;
- the range between minimum and maximum TACH was great, as shown in this diagram.

A case study based on Morogoro in Tanzania compared costs of alternative sanitation improvements.A fully sewered system for the whole town would have cost 1.54 times as much as the recommended combination of sewers for industrial, commercial and public areas with on-site sanitation for residential areas. ®

Costs of the treatment of sewage are often ignored when considering sewerage as an option. In southern Africa it was estimated that conventional treatment would cost over eight times as much as ponds for a population of one thousand. For a population of three thousand the ratio increased to ten unless land was very expensive.®

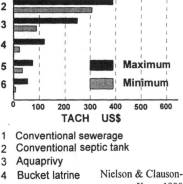

1 Conventional sewerage
2 Conventional septic tank
3 Aquaprivy
4 Bucket latrine   Nielson & Clauson-
5 Compost latrine   Kaas, 1980
6 Pit latrine

Drews, 1983

c. Operation and maintenance

The most important operation to ensure that sanitation is effective is keeping latrines clean. Studies in seven countries showed that latrines may have a negative health effect if they are not properly cleaned and used.®

Attractive prizes and wide media coverage were the reward for the cleanest latrines and drainage in Malawi. The competition was sponsored by a sanitation project to boost the status of owning VIP latrines.®

A survey in two states in India® found that latrines in use formed five roughly equal groups - those that were cleaned every day, two or three times a week, once a week, once a fortnight and once a month. Amongst the reasons given by the 35 per cent of households who did not use their latrines were that pits were full, the pans were choked and there was insufficient water to flush the pans.

In 1978 353 household pit latrines were inspected in Dar es Salaam. Latrines were classified as satisfactory or unsatisfactory on the basis of cleanliness and freedom from unpleasant smell, flies, mosquitoes and cockroaches. It was found that the worst conditions were when all the occupants were tenants. Latrines cleaned by male heads of households

Zacher, 1982

Tukula, 1992
Sinha & Ghosh, 1990

were better than those cleaned by wife or child.

Latrine shelters built of mud or other non-durable material need regular repair, particularly after heavy rain or at the end of the rainy season. Special attention is needed for mud floors, even when they have a skimming of cement mortar. Floors erode more quickly when latrines are used for bathing.

The fly-proof netting at the top of VIP latrine vents is ineffective if it becomes torn by birds or damaged by corrosion. Therefore it should be inspected regularly and replaced if necessary. Inspection is not easy. Some householders have fixed mirrows to the tops of poles so they can see down the vents. Pouring a bucketful of water down a vent pipe that becomes blocked with spiders' webs has been recommended. To avoid the difficulty of getting at the top of a fixed vent to replace netting or clear blockage, pipes can be removeable, fitting in a socket set in the pit slab.

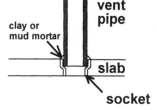

Sullage in pits

Many households which had water connections in Dar es Salaam reported bad nuisance from small, flies and cockroaches. It was probably because more waste water was put into the pits than could infiltrate into the soil. However, in a similar survey which I supervised in unsewered parts of Cairo it was found that vaults into which sullage was tipped were more satisfactory that those only used for excreta.

Morgan, 1988

The advisability of putting sullage into pit latrines is a subject of heated debate. One view® is that VIP latrines 'make excellent washrooms, and they should certainly be used in this way. Water increases the rate of digestion of the contents of the pit. Wet pits last for longer than dry pits'.

Feachem *et al*, 1989

Another authority® wrote 'It is better if the latrine pit is wet and has standing water at the bottom, since this will promote digestion of the wastes and delay the filling of the hole. This can be assisted by plastering the pit floor and bottom part of the pit walls with mortar'. The practice of building bathrooms next to the latrine with wastewater flowing into the pit is common in many countries.® A pit is easier to empty mechanically if the contents are wet.®

Tukula, 1992
Cairncross, 1988

On the other hand, a comment about VIPs in Addis

Ababa® was that 'the main problem ... is that people have been taught to throw excess water down the latrines ... the decomposition principle will not work if additional waste and water are thrown into the tank.' Liquid in a pit with a free water surface can also cause problems with mosquito breeding, as discussed in Section 4b.

Harpham et al, 1988

Hygiene education

Education programmes are often effective in improving cleanliness. In a Tanzanian village, 54 latrines were not clean, but after a hygiene education programme this number dropped to only three.® The programme also resulted in more latrines being fitted with lids, most of which were in place on inspection.

Tanzania, 1984

Evaluation showed that 88 per cent of men involved in a participatory hygiene education programme in Kumasi changed their habits.® Topics included the need to wear shoes when going to a public latrine. Women, who were not involved as it was a muslim area, kept up bad practices. These included leaving latrine doors open, dropping used anal cleaning material in the latrines and spitting on the floor

King & Dinye, 1993

The inside of the shelter of VIP latrines should be kept fairly dark. It is therefore particularly important to keep the door shut, unless the shelter is built with a spiral wall.

After a health education campaign in rural Egyptian villages half the people washed their hands after defecation. ® Where the campaign had not been carried out, only 14 per cent washed hands after using a latrine. A survey in Honduras that covered 1254 latrines found no difference between illiterate and literate people as far as operation and maintenance of latrines was concerned. However, the illiterate people were more receptive to training.® Similarly in nine villages surveyed in Bangladesh no significant relationship was found between literacy and proper use or non-use of latrines.®

El-Katsha & Watts, 1993

Environmental Health, 1993

UNICEF/DPHE, 1980

Controlling nuisance

Many latrine owners are keen to control nuisance from bad smells, flies and mosquitoes. Various materials are put in pits to control smells. Ash is commonly used. If put in while still hot it causes bubbles of gas to explode, which flies do not like! In southern Sudan orange peel is put in

Kotalova, 1984

Wagner & Lanoix, 1958

Skinner, 1994

oil, food or paint tin

mosquito netting

12 mm hole

cone of
mosquito netting

metal sheet
to cover squat hole

Assar, 1971

pit

sacking
soaked
in oil

Morgan & Mara, 1982

pits to control smell — in Bangladesh ash or paddy husk.® In Freetown, Sierra Leone, the owner of a large pit latrine told me that she controlled smells by throwing in waste material when preparing fish for cooking.

A practice that was once common was to add a cupful of kerosene to a wet pit every week to prevent mosquito breeding.® In Uganda some householders set light to a bundle of leaves and put the smoking mass into the pit to kill flies.® Although it kills flies, it also kills their competitors and there may be even more flies later on. Occasional use of insecticide may control Culex mosquitoes in wet pits. However, continuous spraying of pits in Dar es Salaam probably caused insecticide-resistant mosquitoes.

Fly traps over a squat hole are effective against both flies and mosquitoes. They can be made from an empty oil or paint tin with a hole cut in the bottom. Fly-proof netting is fixed across the tin and a cone of netting with a small hole at the apex is fixed inside. A metal sheet that completely covers the remainder of the squat hole is welded or soldered to the tin. Ants soon remove dead flies and mosquitoes.

Insects are sometimes also controlled by fixing sacking soaked in used motor oil draped 300 mm horizontally and 500 mm vertically around sides of pits,® but this is not always effective.

A floating layer of polystyrene beads has been found to be a good way to control mosquitoes in wet pits. The female mosquito cannot lay eggs through the beads and larvae cannot breathe. Polystyrene packing material can be broken up. Pellets can also be obtained. These expand when boiled and remain in place for four years or more. In Tanzania, India and Belize 4.5mm diameter beads were used, but it was later found that a 20mm layer of 2mm beads is better. Tests in Zimbabwe when one kilogram of polystyrene balls were added to a pit reduced the emergence of mosquitoes from about 1500 a week to about 65 a week.®

Dealing with pits

In some regions of Morocco the contents of the belly of a cow or lamb or the head of a lamb are thrown into a newly-dug pit to 'seed' the solids (by introducing microorganisms needed for decomposition).®

Rats are a problem in some pits. Linings with open joints up to ground level are particularly troublesome, as are lining which have not been properly back-filled. I was told in Calcutta that the gases in a well-used pit are a deterrent to rats, but an under-used latrine produces too little gas.

Misuse of twin pit latrines is common unless householders with new latrines are properly instructed. Using both chambers of a double VIP has been reported from Botswana and the twin pits of pour-flush latrines are often used together. I have been told in India, Myanmar, Pakistan and Sri Lanka that many people do not follow the practice of alternate use of pits. When I spoke to several owners of twin pits it was clear they had not been instructed about proper operation.

Leaflets giving instructions about the use and maintenance of latrines were prepared for the Baldia soakpit project in Karachi. It was then realized that most women could not read, so literacy classes were set up. In spite of this, when a consultant surveyed these latrines later almost all of those recorded as 'not in use' had the flow from the latrine or the overflow from the pit redirected to the street open drain.®

It is usual to realize that offset pits are full and need emptying when the pan does not flush. An 'indicator' has been suggested.® This would consist of a piece of wood that slides up and down in a hole in the cover slab. The indicator would be lifted from time to time to see the level of the pit contents. I have never seen this device and think it may provide access for flies and other insects. A similar idea was recommended for septic tanks in South Africa. It was suggested that cloth wrapped round a stick would indicate the depth of sludge and liquor®

There are sometimes distinct local differences in people's willingness to handle excreta. For example one ethnic group in Ghana, the Akans, have a strong objection to dealing with it, even when decomposed.® Another group, the Frafras, have no objection. The Ewe, Gongya and others will handle it when satisfied that it is safe, but not as a paid job as this is looked down upon. In Kenya workmen often empty pits at night because they are ashamed to be seen doing the work.®

Belkhadir, 1990

Bakhteari & Wegelin-Schurunga, 1992

Otis & Mara, 1985

Malan, 1964

Owusu, 1982

Malombe, 1993

Cairncross, 1992

In most places there are not enough tankers to empty all the pits and septic tanks that require the service.® Pits are often neglected because septic tank owners have more political leverage than householders with pits. Wealthy householders with septic tanks may also give tanker crews extra payment to get priority.

The cost of a tanker service is greatly dependent on the distance travelled between collection points and the place where tankers discharge. ® For large tankers, such as the Brevac, saving can be achieved by emptying several pits or tanks that are close together.

Williams, 1987

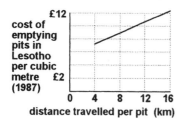

cost of emptying pits in Lesotho per cubic metre (1987)

distance travelled per pit (km)

When tankers were used for emptying pits in Karachi householders paid for the service and found that at a single visit the tanker could empty both chambers of double pits. So some householders used both chambers until they were full and then had both emptied at the same time. When pits were full, some householders called in private masons. The masons often proposed additional expensive and totally unnecessary work, such as making an overflow to an open · drain or building a third chamber for double pits.

Water seals and sewer connections

Advice sometimes given to keep pour-flush latrines in good condition is to pour a little water into the pan before defecation to prevent faeces sticking. Blocked traps can be freed by tying rag round a stick and moving it up and down in the water in the pan with a pumping action. Traps over pits (the 'gooseneck' type) are often broken by too vigorous efforts to clear a blockage. In nine villages surveyed in Bangladesh® about a quarter of goosenecks were deliberately holed to avoid blockage.

UNICEF/DPHE, 1980

People newly connected to sewerage systems often need instruction in their proper use. Otherwise blockage by unsuitable anal cleaning material such as newspaper often occurs. Non-conventional sewerage requires a strong organization for maintenance.® Regular de-sludging of household interceptor chambers is especially important. Without de-sludging these chambers become full of grit and sludge. When chambers are full of solids there is no retention of liquids, solids pass straight through with no settlement. The chambers then fail to achieve their purpose, which is to ensure that solids do not block small diameter sewers.

Wegelin-Schurunga, 1991

Chapter 9: COMMUNITY EFFORTS

a. Community management, motivation and mobilization

Communities and participation

A GROUP OF people, whether living in a few isolated dwellings, or in a village, or in part of a town or city, may already have or may develop a cohesiveness that justifies the title of 'community'. The sense of community is increased by carrying out some activity together and by participating in joint ventures.

Many definitions of 'community participation' have been suggested. One nearly forty years ago was 'the participation by the people themselves in efforts to improve their level of living with as much reliance as possible on their own initiative; and the provision of technical and other services in ways which encourage initiative, self-help and mutual help and make these more effective'.® Even politicians share this idea. The President of Zambia wrote 'the people should be given the opportunity to participate at every level in the formulation of policy and the running of their affairs'.®

United Nations, 1956

Kaunda, 1972

A more recent comment was 'it is the local people themselves, not those trying to help them, who have the most important role. The community itself must be the primary decision maker, the primary investor, the primary maintainer, the primary organizer, and the primary overseer'.® Consequently, communities' responsibilities may be to *manage* their own schemes as well as participating in programmes in which governments, donors and voluntary agencies also play a part. Community management occurs when the beneficiaries of services have responsibility, authority and control of their services.®

Briscoe & Ferranti, 1988

Chauhan *et al*, 1983

Communities working together

A common practice in part of Uganda is for a family that wants a latrine to brew beer, cook food and invite the neighbouring men to help dig. About ten friends turn up, dig the pit to a depth of about five metres in the day and then enjoy the feast.®

Begamuhunda, 1991

In Baldia, the large *katchi abadi* in Karachi, the sanitation programme around 1980 consisted of construction of pour-flush latrines and lined pits. Early in the programme eleven members of a cricket team, including a mason, were keen to improve sanitation so they could practice in the streets which had previously been blocked by the tops of soakpits. In a month they dug pits and built latrines within plots for ten households, and then continued to build many more.®

Ain, 1981

In Tanzania villagers chose how to reward masons who built latrines. In three out of a group of four villages the masons were paid cash. In the fourth village the masons were exempted from their normal village tasks. Elsewhere people who were provided with latrines worked on the farms of masons during the construction period.®

Wright, 1982

SanPlat slabs are available in Malawi when a production team moves into a village in which a required percentage of households have dug pits. To get enough pits dug the most enthusiastic villagers persuade their less-active neighbours to dig.®

Cairncross, 1992

The village of Nyamori in Tanzania provided a good example of cooperative effort in 1976. Each family unit had to dig a pit nine metres deep. A hundred and fifty out of two hundred and seventy five families in the village dug their pits in the first two weeks of April. They also collected locally-available material for fabrication of slabs and shelters. Apart from making concrete slabs, all the work was organized and carried out by the villagers themselves.®

Kalimanzila, 1980

Promotion and motivation

Gibbs, 1984
Elmendorf & Buckles, 1980
Samanta, 1993
Narayan-Parker, 1985
Tobin, 1985

Latrine construction, maintenance and use has been promoted in many programmes for improving water supplies, including those in Bangladesh,® Guatemala,® India,® the Maldives® and Nepal.®

In the Nawal Parasi Hill Project, Nepal, drinking water schemes were only implemented after every household had constructed a latrine. Latrine construction was seen as an organizational test for a village. Local leaders able to mobilize their communities to build latrines were expected to be better able to manage the construction and maintenance of their water systems. ®

Williamson, 1983

A survey revealed that the inhabitants of Bhaktapur in Nepal, few of whom had latrines, considered themselves to be healthy. A film show on sanitation-related diseases was given and then people were invited to bring in their stools. Most had worms and saw them under a microscope. A deworming campaign was launched. The prize for most worms was won by a seven-year-old girl who produced sixty-three worms in three sittings. People realized that they had to take action themselves. Within five days a delegation went to the project office to seek help, sites for demonstration latrines had been selected, material had been collected, pits dug and construction of latrines had started. ®

Lohani & Guhr, 1985

Community participation was encouraged in Trinidad and Tobago by inviting members of the public to propose slogans on ways of improving environmental health.®

Thomas & Ramamurthy, 1984

It was claimed that the increase of latrine use in Bangladesh from 4 per cent to 25 per cent between 1985 and 1992 was due to the motivation programme being based on privacy, convenience, comfort of women and prestige rather than health.®

IRC Newsletter, 1992

Promotional campaigns were tailored to local circumstances in a rural sanitation project in the Philippines.® In some villages help was obtained from organizations like Lions clubs, religious groups and mothers' clubs. Toilet bowls were provided free of charge and households dug and lined pits and built wooden platforms and shelters.

McCommon *et al*, 1990

In the early 1990s the Government of India allocated ten per cent of the funds for the central rural sanitation programme to 'information, education and communication' (IEC). IEC cells were set up in several states.®

Drawings, slides, films and videos are often used to put over the importance of latrines, how to build them and how to use them properly. However, 'audio-visual materials are no substitute for group discussions and activities'.® In some places drama and dance are popular activities for hygiene promotion. I have seen groups dancing round their villages singing their own vernacular songs extolling the virtues of good sanitation. In Zimbabwe explanation of the principles of VIP latrines was included in the primary school syllabus.®

Samanta, 1993

MacGarry, 1983

Burgers *et al*, 1988

Promotion of sanitation is sometimes difficult. Communities, like individuals, may see little advantage in building latrines. In the west of Nepal a latrine promotion

Paudyal, 1992

campaign met stiff resistance until a man was killed by a bear while defecating by himself in the jungle.®

Community committees

Agencies often require, or encourage, the formation of committees to run sanitation projects. The membership of committees is sometimes defined, for example by requiring a minimum number of women members. Minority groups may also be given representatives on committees.

Davis *et al*, 1993

Often committees are set up to deal with both water and sanitation, but sometimes one committee deals with sanitation and another committee with water. There is a danger of too many committees, leading to confusion. In Ethiopia during the 1980s some villages had up to twelve committees. These might include committees for development, health, water, sanitation and youth. Others ran community shops or producers' cooperatives.®

Demonstration latrines

Another facet of many sanitation mobilization campaigns is building a few demonstration latrines. These may be built at the homes of trained masons or members of the mobilization team. In some villages the chief's 'palace' is selected. In a pilot sanitation programme in Ghana the religious Imam in one village built three latrines to find out

Davis et al, 1993

which was the best design.® Political leaders are sometimes selected for the honour of having a demonstration latrine at their homes. Other sites are village halls and political party headquarters. However, latrines at such places may only be open during office hours and if not properly cared for are not a good recommendation for household latrines.

Watt & Laing, 1985

A good way to demonstrate how a VIP latrine works was used in Zimbabwe.® Small model latrines were made from cardboard boxes, with jam jars representing the pits. Then smouldering (not flaming) newspaper was put in the jars. The smoke represented smells. In the model simple pit smoke came out of the squat hole, but it went up the vent shaft of the VIP when wind blew through the entrance. Then live flies were put in the jam jars. They flew out of the squat hole of the simple pit. In the VIP they disappeared up the vent pipe.

Unsatisfactory   demonstration   latrines   are   no recommendation. In Baluchistan two dry pit latrines were built.® They did not work properly and were rejected by the community. Pour-flush latrines were then tried but had flushing and splashing problems. Naturally, the demand for latrines declined until a better pan was available.

Pasha & McGarry, 1989

Appropriate technology for community participation

Some of the success of the Lesotho rural sanitation programme in the mid 1980s was attributed to the use of a technology which had been proved elsewhere. VIP latrines were known to have been effective in neighbouring Zimbabwe. More than six hundred VIPs were built in the district of Mohale's Hoek in Lesotho during a three-year project period, against a target of four hundred. By accepting the known technology the project was able to concentrate on 'broader software issues, such as community participation and health and hygiene education'.® Training of latrine builders was a major part of the Lesotho rural sanitation programme. One of the trained local builders was a woman who actively marketed her skills by going house to house and speaking with local chiefs.

UNDP-World Bank, 1990

A builders' manual for VIP latrines was produced in Zimbabwe after a background survey showed that local builders were unclear about such important details as the height of the vent pipe and the thickness of the slab.® The draft manual, with step by step instructions, was given to some builders. The authors watched whether the builders followed the instructions well and easily. This exposed many errors in the draft — errors that were corrected for the published version. This experience led to suggestions that there should be four stages in the production of information..

Laver, 1986

1. Identify common construction problems in villages;
2. investigate knowledge levels and ideas of building in villages;
3. examine how the community sees the need for improved sanitation;
4. develop appropriate methods of communicating information.®

Laver, 1988

In some projects where emphasis has been placed on community participation and hygiene education, latrine builders have been made responsible for imparting health

Cairncross, 1989

Tobin, 1985

Samanta, 1993

Pasha & McGarry, 1989

McGilvray, 1984

Franceys, 1991

information. This may not be the best way to proceed as quite different skills are required.® In Nepal the training of technicians included hygiene education. This was not done so that they themselves would be health educators, but rather that they should be properly motivated and so pass on this motivation.®

Affordable participation

It is sometimes difficult to decide who should get encouragement and help in latrine construction. The poorest people obviously need most help, but providing household latrines may be inappropriate for squatters. In Zimbabwe very low cost VIPs were developed but it was then found that they did not last long and maintenance costs were higher than the more expensive versions. It has been suggested that poor people follow the example of better-off neighbours who build latrines. Conversely, if subsidies help poor people to have latrines, those who can afford it do not want to be 'outdone by poor people', so pay for latrines themselves.®

In the Mansehra District of Pakistan, demonstration latrines were unsuccessful in motivating communities to build their own latrines. The cost was too high for the people living in this mountainous area. Too high costs were also blamed for the poor implementation rate in the Punjab Sanitation Programme, where less than a third of the planned latrines were installed. Many latrines that were built had oversize pits and elaborate shelters.®

Protracted participation

One of the problems with involving communities is delay. ® 'It takes longer to grow new crops than to eat a meal; it takes longer to . . build latrines than to treat a case of dysentery; and much longer again for villagers to learn the necessity for them and how to use and maintain them'.

Often when agencies manage projects and programmes the work starts well because expertise and resources are readily available. After the agency has completed its input the benefits usually decrease. The project becomes less effective. With a community in charge the start is slow because the enthusiasm and effort have to be built up.® However, the work, and hence the benefits of community run projects, are likely to be more sustainable, so that eventually the achievements are greater than for an agency-run scheme, as shown here.

Communities and professionals

A review of several successful projects asked 'who are the men and women who make community water, sanitation and health projects work?' and concluded that 'contrary to the popular image, the key persons are dedicated professionals rather than unpaid volunteers .. These professionals .. were the vital link between the community and the government. They were the primary motivators, usually salaried project staff'.®

It is important to take social factors into account when embarking on sanitation programmes. However, Chambers ® claims that many social anthropologists have been unable or unwilling to give practical advice. Asked for suggestions about what to do, they might give replies on the lines of 'give me five years and I will tell you why I need longer before I can tell you why you should proceed with the utmost caution'. Nevertheless, many projects and programmes have been greatly helped by sociological inputs. Extension workers with a sociological bckground are often able to gain the confidence of communities, who then work with technical staff to construct and sustain sanitation facilities.

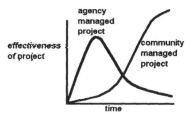

Chauhan *et al*, 1983

Chambers, 1983

b. Help from agencies

In spite of the advantages of communities managing their own sanitation improvement programmes, most latrine construction depends to greater or lesser extent on the assistance of outside agencies. The *agency* may be a government department, a donor or an NGO.

Help with 'software'

The help given by agencies may be restricted to advising communities or individual householders. In the Zezencho area of southern Ethiopia an agency introduced good sanitation and hygiene practices and the concept of pit latrines.® The agency did not build the latrines, but responded to requests to help form committees consisting of four women who organized households to dig pits. The agency trained artisans to help the villagers build latrines,

Davis *et al*, 1993

which were affordable, using no outside building materials. The idea of building latrines soon spread.

In some states in India the government in collaboration with UNICEF have set up 'rural sanitation marts'. These are retail outlets for materials required. Panels of trained masons help householders build their own latrines.®

Samanta, 1993

Because of the communal benefit of individual's sanitation practices, many agencies conduct hygiene education or hygiene promotion programmes.® These may be part of a latrine promotion campaign. Sometimes the objective is instruction in proper use and maintenance of latrines, as discussed in Chapter 8.

Niedrum, 1993;
    Dennis-Antwi, 1993

Paying all the cost

The agency's assistance in Zezencho mentioned above was important, but was confined to software. It was not involved in construction of latrines. On the other hand, some agencies' projects include all preparatory work and cover the entire cost of building latrines. There are also many examples of agencies who spend more than is necessary and resist adopting low cost methods, due to some of the following reasons:®

Amos, 1993

- they are unwilling to adopt standards that are inferior to those in developed countries;
- professionals are reluctant to prepare schemes they regard as inferior to best practice;
- external funding agencies often insist on standards which they consider will protect their investment;
- innovative schemes require substantial research and design investment and have more risk than conventional designs.

There is a long-standing argument as the whether on-site sanitation is a proper sphere for assistance from public funds. Some local and central governments maintain that providing latrines should be the entire responsibility of the owners or tenants of dwellings. On the other hand, as discussed in Chapter 2, good sanitation is a 'public good' because lack of sanitation has an adverse effect on people other than those living in a dwelling without a latrine. Gradually the understanding of agencies and working together is being better understood. Public good is related to agencies' hygiene promotion activities, with householders undertaking the physical work.

Subsidies

Many governments and donors assist with 'below the feet' construction of latrines — perhaps giving (or selling at a subsidized price) material for linings and floor slabs or for pour-flush pans, and sometimes paying labour to dig pits. Householders are then responsible for the shelter - the 'above the feet' construction.

In the past the government in India at both state and federal level allocated large sums as subsidy for those constructing latrines or converting dry latrines to the pour-flush twin pit variety.

The contribution varied greatly. The central government gave a 40 per cent subsidy. In Andhra Pradesh the state paid the entire balance. Several state governments paid another 40 per cent, leaving 20 per cent to be met by the beneficiary. The state's contribution was 20 per cent in Kerala and 50 per cent in Maharashtra. In West Bengal and Manipur the State paid for 60 per cent of the below-slab costs, leaving the beneficiaries to cover 60 per cent of the cost of the shelter.®

WHO/SEARO, 1988

In the early 1990s it was realized that even massive budgets would only go a little way to solve the problem because thirteen million households were without adequate sanitation. The subsidy was therefore confined to the poorest groups.®

Samanta, 1993

A different system for providing subsidy applied in Botswana. When the householder had dug and lined the pit, the authority provided a pre-cast concrete slab, ventilation pipe, toilet seat and lid, blocks, door, door frame, cement and labour for completing a VIP latrine, all for the equivalent of £15 in 1992.®

Mpowe, 1992

The number of latrines in Mozambique increased twenty-fold between 1970 and 1984. At first the city council of Maputo provided latrines free of charge in selected areas of the city. The free issue did nothing to encourage other people to build their own latrines. Progress was made when twelve cooperatives were formed. Each cooperative had eight trained people who made the domed unreinforced slabs described in Chapter 4. Each slab had the maker's signature, so those who made defective slabs could be identified and retrained or boycotted. A handcart was acquired so customers could take their purchases home.®

Brandberg, 1983

Governments

Governments have been conspicuous in providing latrines that have *not* been what local people want. Old reports from Nyasaland (now Malawi) make interesting reading.® In

Nyasaland, various dates

1938 it was 'unusual to find a village without at least one latrine', but 'in many cases latrines are provided by the population mainly to conform with regulations and not for use'. Ten years later it was reported that 'latrines tend to be regarded as objects to show rather than conveniences to use'. Because government officers ordered villagers to dig latrines, *not* having a latrine became a sign of political integrity in the struggle for independence.

This attitude to government activity still exists. Not long ago a report from rural Bangladesh commented that people think that anything to do with the government or

Chadha & Strauss, 1991

outside agencies must be a complex affair.® Local regulations and byelaws often justify this criticism (they are discussed in the next section).

In Latin America, contracts for construction of latrines were drawn up between health departments and householders. However, this took the health staff a lot of time. In south-east Asia it was customary for health staff to help respected leaders of communities to install latrines so that possession of latrines became associated with positions

Wagner & Lanoix, 1958

of prestige in the communities.®

To accustom people to VIP latrines in Kenya the Ministry of Health imported stainless steel flyproof netting. To renew a licence, licensed premises are required to either

Wegelin-Schuringa, 1991

upgrade existing latrines or build a new VIP.®

Donors

In Bangladesh UNICEF provided a 60% subsidy on the sale of units consisting of a concrete slab and one concrete ring,

Wan, 1992

made at one thousand village sanitation centres In the Norad programme in Zimbabwe, village health workers were trained in latrine construction and provided with materials for two latrines, one at their own homes and one

Boydell, 1990

at a central point in the village.®

In Myanmar the intervention of UNICEF in the national sanitation programme increased coverage from 12

Rosenhall, 1990

per cent in 1982 to 27 per cent in 1988.® Seven hundred thousand latrines were built, most of which used HDP pans provided by UNICEF at a cost of $7 per person.

In the *katchi abadi* of Baldia in Karachi various types of
pour-flush latrines were built. Between 1979 and 1985 the
cost of 1065 demonstration latrines was covered by
UNICEF and other agencies.® By 1985, about fourteen
thousand households had household latrines. So latrines
provided by donors resulted in thirteen times as many
latrines built at owners' expense.

Pasha & McGarry, 1989

NGOs and the private sector

Twenty years ago a report concluded that 'the unique value
of voluntary agencies is neither the resources they generate
from the private sector nor the programmes they fund and
implement. Rather it is their ability to see things in a
different light than the public sector and their courage in
giving voice to this difference'.®

US AID, 1973

In Bolivia NGOs were selected to undertake the work
under contract after the failure of government departments
to implement US AID-funded sanitation programmes.®

Karp, 1992

A resettled community in Colombo tried to organize
infrastructural improvements on their own. When they met
the authority they were showered with promises that were
never fulfilled. So they gave up until a few Buddhist and
Christian clergymen living in the neighbourhood discussed
the problems with the people, took up their case, presented
petitions and eventually got the work done.®

Etherton, 1980

A much-publicized example of community
management is in the largest *katchi abadi* in Karachi.® The
Orangi Pilot Project (OPP) has resulted in the construction
of many kilometres of low cost sewerage. 'Lane managers'
have been appointed by lane committees and receive no
pay. They collect contributions from householders in the
lane, which is the unit of operation. The lane managers
make arrangements for purchase of materials or for
contractors to construct the sewers. OPP staff give advice
and supervise construction when requested. During my
several visits to Orangi since 1979 — most recently in 1993
— I have seen the extension of low cost sewers to most of
the area.

Khan, 1992

Like many other visitors to Safai Vidyalaya, the NGO
that Ishwardhai Patel founded, I have been amazed at his
continuing enthusiasm over many years. His first efforts to
promote pour-flush latrines in Ahmedabad, India, failed
completely. With fifteen co-workers he tried to persuade

people to accept free latrines. Nobody wanted one. Then one old lady asked to have a latrine. Within two weeks of building her latrine over a hundred applicants came forward.®

In many countries NGOs are playing a major role in encouraging and supporting the construction of latrines. For example, in 1982 the NGO Forum for drinking water supply and sanitation in Bangladesh established 183 village sanitation centres to produce latrine slabs and pit lining rings.®

Some NGOs help householders to operate and maintain their latrines. Bodies like Sulabh International and Safai Vidyaley in India give support during the crucial early months after latrine construction until householders become accustomed to the responsibility of ownership.

There is currently a strong move in many developing countries towards greater involvement of the private sector in public works.® Some studies have concluded that employees in the private sector are more efficient than those working for government departments. Reasons given for a government's inefficiency include their employees' greater job security, the lack of incentive systems, inflexible use of staff and absence of linkage between productivity and salaries.® Budget constraints also prevent government agencies from adopting cost-cutting technologies, and decision-making is motivated by a need to avoid public controversy. However, privatization reduces employment and staff welfare. Unprofitable activities may be neglected even if socially desirable.

c. Regulations, control and planning

Inappropriate regulations

In most Third World cities, non-compliance with by-laws and planning ordinances is commonplace.® 'In spite of the overwhelming difficulty which most governments have in providing and maintaining city services, they tend to retain and enforce regulations and standards which, in most instances, were set under very different circumstances'.®

One common example is the requirement that all new dwellings must have water closets connected to sewers. This ignores the fact that the majority of new houses are built in peri-urban areas and may be miles away from

Charnock, 1983

NGO Forum, 1993

Morris, 1993

Raj, 1991

Lowder, 1986

Anstee, 1990

sewers. A slightly more sensible requirement is that new dwellings must have a WC discharging to a septic tank if there is no nearby sewer. But this ignores the common lack of piped water. Often only small amounts of water are available for flushing because all water has to be carried from distant standposts, wells or streams. Then WCs are likely to become health and environmental nuisances.

Pit latrines are often illegal. For example, the by-laws for Kibera (a fair-sized city ten kilometres from Nairobi) ban pit latrines. A local NGO, KWAHO, ignored the by-laws and built twenty thousands VIP latrines and then organized an emptying service.®

Munyakho, 1992

Responsible authorities

In Lesotho the urban and rural sanitation programmes operated under different Ministries and were supported by different donors. Nevertheless there was close liaison which resulted in standardization of concrete slabs, common publicity campaigns and joint training.®

Blackett, 1988

Some countries, like Brazil and Tunisia, created financially autonomous agencies for water supply and sanitation.® It has been quite common in other countries to form 'boards' or other bodies which are legally autonomous although the financial autonomy is pointless because any deficit is automatically picked up by the state or national government.

UNCHS, 1989

Ad hoc institutions are often set up to deal with an externally-funded project. In many of these cases no funds are available when the project is completed and the institution and its staff are left high and dry.

Master plans

In the past, master plans prepared by expatriate consultants were notorious for adherence to standards appropriate for the industrialized countries from which the consultants came. Gradually during the late 1970s and the 1980s master plans gave at least notional attention to low cost sanitation, just as they did to community participation, training and other 'software' issues. For example, consultants for Chittagong proposed sewers for central areas with piped water supply, on-site sanitation for other areas and communal latrines for central areas where premises had no piped supply.®

Moes & Zwagg, 1984

d. Public and communal latrines

Strictly speaking, 'communal latrines' are those outside
household plots that are used by people for their daily
needs when at home. 'Public latrines' are in or near
markets, lorry parks and the like and are intended for
people away from their homes.® However, this distinction
is not always observed, so 'public' is used here for both
types. Latrines for schools and other institutions are in
some ways similar to public latrines (see Section 9e).

Pickford, 1991

Public latrines have been provided since ancient times.
In AD 315 there were more than a hundred and forty public
latrines in the city of Rome.® Many had been built several
centuries BC.® At about the same time terracotta covers
were provided for pit latrines at Vaishali in Bihar, India.
Public latrines were not uncommon there.®

Harris, 1990
Wilcocks, 1965

Many villages in Ghana have large communal pit
latrines, often with the women's latrine on one side of the
village and men's on the other. They are usually roofed in
thatch or palm leaves and have either completely open sides
or dwarf walls. A common additional feature is small pits
for children near to the adult latrines. A Ghanaian survey in
the late 1970s showed the importance of these latrines. 137
villages had 387 communal latrines.®

Misra, 1988

Wright et al, 1978

Normally public latrines consist of cubicles side-by-
side. A two-thousand-year-old Roman latrine can still be
seen at Timgad in North Africa. Twenty-five stone seats,
each separated from the next by a carved dolphin, are
grouped around three sides of a large room, in the middle
of which a fountain once played.® In the Middle Ages 'a
fair large house' was provided as a latrine for the monks at
Durham, England. There were partitions between the seats
'very decent so that one of them could not see one another,
when they were in that place'.®

Reynolds, 1943

Lambton, 1978

Separate sections with their own entrances are usually
provided for men and women. Exceptionally the six-sided
aqua privy communal latrines built in the 1970s in Calcutta
were single chambers which were used by both men and
women. They were planned at a rate of one for every 25
people.® This follows an Indian rule for communal latrines
based on an average of seven-and-a-half minutes for
defecation over three hours when the latrines are used in the
mornings.

Maitra, 1978

A 1982 IDA-approved design for Monrovia grouped 50 to 75 people to share a centrally-located 'wet core' located along roads or footpaths. Each was to have twelve cubicles, shower units, standpipes and outside lights, each cubicle having its own access and a lockable door.®

The Urban Edge, 1982

An interesting latrine was built at Gopeshwar in the Himalayan foothills during 1984-5. Designed by the Uttar Pradesh Jal Nigam, it consisted of seventeen cubicles facing outwards around a biogas chamber.®

Sagar & Chourasia, 1990

Public latrines built in Tema, Ghana, during the 1980s consisted of cubicles side by side with squatting slabs set over 200mm diameter pipes. One pipe was for eight men's toilets and urinals. The other had eleven women's toilets. Tanks at the upper ends of the pipes filled continuously with water and tipped automatically when full, flushing solids along the pipes to a nearby sewer.®

Amoaning-Yankson, 1983

A similar system was used in the 1970s when the UK charity Oxfam developed communal latrines for Bangladesh that could be erected quickly in refugee camps. Flow from ten or more pans was flushed to butyl rubber tanks, where it was retained for about two weeks.® However the objective of reducing cholera vibrio was only partially successful.®

Howard, 1977

Daniel & Lloyd, 1980

Many mosques have communal latrines, which may be the only provision for men — women being left to their own devices. Christian churches also provided latrines. John Wesley in 1769 advised his followers 'I particularly desire wherever you have preaching . . that there may be a little house'.®

Pudney, 1984

Unsatisfactory public latrines

Public latrines as an alternative to household latrines in congested areas are rarely satisfactory. In the 1950s it was reported that 'in most instances communal latrines, irrespective of the type of design, proved to be failures'.® In 1990, 71 per cent of those who used public latrines in Kumasi were not satisfied with them.® In rural India only 5% of people have access to public latrines, but of these only one in ten actually use them.®

Wagner & Lanoix, 1958

Whittington et al, 1992

GOI, 1990

The trouble with public latrines everywhere is operation and maintenance. In 1914 the City Engineer of Bombay wrote 'no matter what accommodation is provided, fouling of the roads in the neighbourhood of

'Turner, 1914

Marais, 1973

Dewit & Schenk, 1986

Ilustre, 1980

Nwokocha, 1990

[public] latrines and urinals always take place. The inside of urinals and latrines is not only misused, but the outside as well'.® The two most important reasons for unsatisfactory public latrines are lighting and cleanliness. Misuse is more likely if there is not adequate lighting at night. If possible lighting should also be provided along the path to the latrine.®

Once a latrine is fouled, subsequent users have no alternative but to foul it more. A major problem is usually who is to keep the latrine clean.

Maintenance is also a problem. In 1988 a study was made of a Madras slum-upgrading project that had included construction of latrines.® In one upgraded slum four out of the seven communal latrines built in 1980 were permanently out of order. So 30 per cent of the people had again resorted to open defecation.

Over-use of public latrines is common. The situation is often made worse because in areas with expanding populations the authorities are unwilling to build more latrines because of their bad reputation. In Manila a study in the late 1970s found that one latrine with four seats for women and four for men, which was originally intended for 200 people, was being used by 3000 people daily.®

Popular public latrines

The problem of cleaning can be overcome if the community genuinely wants a communal latrine, contributes to its construction and plans cleaning before construction starts. In the small town of Afikpo in eastern Nigeria the whole community agreed to build a communal latrine, an alternating VIP with 22 cubicles. ® The young men cleared the site. Women collected sand and gravel for construction. A regular levy was raised — a large piece of yam from men, a measure of rice from the women. These were sold, the proceeds paying for other material.

For multi-compartment alternating VIP latrines the lined pit is divided into sections, one more section of the pit than the number of compartments. The sections are used alternately. Sections at the ends each take excreta from one compartment, but other sections are twice as large as they take excreta from two adjoining compartments. At first pit section A takes excreta from compartment 1, C from compartments 2 and 3 and E from compartment 4. After a year or more, section B takes excreta from compartments 1 and 2 and section D from compartments 3 and 4. When the second set of pit sections are nearly full the decomposed excreta in the first set can be taken out without risk of disease or nuisance from smell. Many multi-compartment alternating latrines have been built in West Africa.® and elsewhere.

Lochery & Adu-Asah, no date

In Manila, local residents had to register, and pay a registration fee, to use communal latrines and laundry facilities. The fees were enough to pay for metered water and for other operation and maintenance costs. In Nepal a shop was attached to a communal latrine. Instead of paying rent the shopkeeper had to keep the latrine clean.®

WEDC, 1988

If communal latrines are to be kept clean, attendants should be paid by the community. Government (or local government) servants may not do the job properly if they are paid the same whether the latrines are clean or filthy.® Attendants should be present whenever large latrines are in use. A 1868 report about public latrines in Cawnpore (Kanpur) in India noted that a separate residence was provided for the sweepers (attendants) 'so that they need never be absent'.®

Wegelin-Schuringa, 1991

Harrison, 1980

In Indonesia some village heads made lists of people selected by their families to clean and maintain the MCK during the next week ['mandi' = bathing; 'cuci' = cleaning and 'kakus' = toilet]. The head checked the work. Families who participate can use the MCK free of charge, and contribute to the cost of de-sludging the septic tank.®

de Kruijff, 1986

In Ibadan in the late 1960s several communal latrines called 'comfort stations' were built. The smallest served 200-300 people and had ten latrine cubicles, eight shower cubicles and a laundry room. Excreta and waste water passed to a two-chamber tank with a capacity of more than fifty cubic metres.® The first chamber was under the latrine compartments, so the comfort stations were strictly aqua privies. The comfort stations involved a considerable amount of community participation® but did not prove sustainable. Water and electricity had been cut off from most of the comfort stations because of non-payment of bills when I visited Ibadan in the mid 1980s .

Oluyemi, 1972

Pasteur, 1979

These comfort stations were improved versions of public latrines common in west African towns and villages. In Kumasi about 60 per cent of the public latrines were of

Communal aqua privy latrine

this type in 1991. They are locally known as 'bombers' because the accumulation of methane occasionally explodes due to the not uncommon practice of smoking to counteract unpleasant smells in badly maintained latrines. In 1990 there were about 400 public (or communal) latrines scattered throughout Kumasi, used by about 40 per cent of households. About 60 per cent of them were aqua-privies, 25 per cent were bucket latrines and there were a few KVIPs and WCs discharging to septic tanks.

Whittington et al, 1992

Charging for use

Exceptions to the general dissatisfaction with public latrines are new latrines for which users pay private or communal contractors. The idea is not new. At the 1851 Great Exhibition in London's Hyde Park 827,280 people (14 per cent of the visitors) paid for use of public toilets.®

Wright, 1960

In Kumasi at all public latrines in the city centre and about half of the communal latrines elsewhere adults are charged for using latrines. Children and the elderly are admitted free.® In 1992 the charge was five cedis (about one and a half US cents) for the old pan latrines, but was ten cedis for better-kept KVIPs and twenty cedis for new latrines with WCs. Charges were made for many public latrines throughout Ghana. Collection of fees is made at ticket booths to attendants who collect the money and give each person a piece of newspaper for anal cleaning. In 1993 I revisited a large latrine in Sekondi, in the Western Region of Ghana (I had built it 35 years before when I was Town Engineer there). In 1993 the charge for use was ten cedis (about three US cents).

Whittington *et al*, 1992

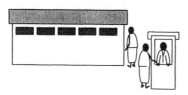

Operation by contractors

By 1993 Sulabh International had built and were maintaining more than 2500 sanitation complexes in India. They operate on the 'pay and use´ principle and most include showers or other washing facilities as well as latrines. The usual charge was one rupee (about four US cents) for the latrine and one-and-a-half rupees (about six US cents) for use of the shower. No charge was made for urinals. The appearance of some complexes was made attractive, with greenery planted around the buildings.

Ribeiro, 1985

The first Sulabh latrine was built for the Municipal Corporation of Patna, Bihar.® Operation and maintenance was covered by a pay-and-use contract with Sulabh. The Council paid water and electricity charges. The unit had thirty cubicles and included bathing rooms, wash basins and taps for washing clothes. Women, children and invalids did not have to pay and no charge was made for men to use urinals, which had separate access. I saw this first Sulabh latrine in 1978 and have since inspected several fine Sulabh public latrines in other Indian cities.

Waste from a communal latrine with 54 places constructed by Sulabh at Patna in 1982 fed an underground digester that produced about 55 cubic metres of biogas a day. It was originally intended to use the gas for domestic cooking and heating, but the plan was changed. Gas was passed to an engine powering a 10kVA generator. This gave electricity to light the complex, an adjoining park and street lights along four kilometres of a busy city road.

In Kumasi in the early 1990s, some good latrines were built by the Metropolitan Assembly and then maintained by private contractors under a franchise system. Following competitive bidding the contractors paid monthly fees to the Assembly and collected fees from the users. The advantage of these systems, which also exist in other countries, is that the contractor knows that his income from users will drop if the standard of cleanliness falls.

In Lagos operation and maintenance of public latrines by contractors was tried, but was not successful. However, in the mid 1980s the fees were sufficient to cover the costs of the attendant, toilet paper, soap and water for hand washing, and cleaning materials. ®

Lochery & Adu-Asah, no date

In the 1970s the market cooperative in Chawama, a squatter suburb of Lusaka, used fees from stallholders to pay the City Council for cleaning the public latrines.®

Muller, 1988

During a visit to Bangladesh I was told about a franchise latrine in Chittagong. Piped water was connected so that the contractor could clean the latrine and provide users with water for anal cleaning. At one time the piped supply failed and the contractor (to maintain his income from users) hired men to carry water from a distant source.

e. School latrines

Sanitation programmes often include the construction of latrines for schools. Children are more at risk than adults from excreta-related diseases, especially roundworms. Good hygiene practices can be learned at school and some children who get into the habit of using latrines at school persuade parents to build them at home.

Building school latrines has not always achieved these objectives. A report of a project at Kwale in Kenya® makes a point that the school latrine was only used by teachers. Unfortunately this is not unusual. I have seen many school latrines in various countries in Africa and Asia where the teachers lock the only latrine, keeping it for their own use while the children relieve themselves around the school playground or by a boundary fence. Experience in Lesotho taught the responsible agency the importance of commitment of schools to 'proper use, care and maintenance of hygienic sanitation facilities'.®

Cairncross, 1992

Khaketla et al, 1986

WHO, 1951

More than forty years ago, a WHO Expert Committee® commented that children learn harmful habits which may never be eradicated if school latrines are dirty. A well-built and well-kept pit latrine may be far safer and give better training than a tiled WC which is allowed to become dirty and a nuisance.

A thorough survey of all existing school latrines was carried out before designing a new type of latrine block for use in crowded urban school sites in Blantyre, Malawi.® Amongst the features found to be important for cleanliness were making the inside of the building as light as possible and restricting the size of cubicles and passages. If there is too much space, children tend to defecate in corners rather than down the squat hole. Good drainage is essential so that the floor can be regularly cleaned and good ventilation ensures that wet floors dry.

Abel & Dohrman, 1993

Aqua privy latrines were built for schools by Umgeni Water in South Africa.® Early trouble with fly breeding cured itself when digestion of excreta in the tank became fully established. All stages of decision-making were shared between the school staff, parents' committees and the school inspectorate. Unemployed parents undertook all work except supervision.

Burgess, 1993

The pits for latrines built for schools in Nepal had a volume of six cubic metres.® This was based on between seventy and one hundred children using each latrine. It was estimated that the pits would last three to five years, with sludge accumulating at 20 litres per user per year.

Strauss, 1983

Chapter 10: SELECTION, EVALUATION AND UPGRADING

a. Guides for selection

INDIVIDUAL HOUSEHOLDERS OR communities should have the greatest possible freedom to select what they want. However, technological considerations may lead logically to a particular type, or a few types, of sanitation. A 1993 consultation in south-east Asia commented, 'no technology should be chosen for a community by outsiders. Outsiders should first study what communities are currently doing, and then seek to build upon existing practices, making improvements that are affordable at each step.'®

WHO/SEARO, 1993

Even when one type of technology is favoured, householders can still be given a genuine choice as in the Rama Krishna Mission programme in West Bengal.® In Zimbabwe a range of spiral VIP latrines was offered in 1990. The cheapest had a thatched roof shelter and used one bag of cement. Others used two, three or four bags.

Huda, 1993

Several years ago twenty-five types of rural latrine were reviewed at an international meeting.® Weightings were given to twenty-six attributes. Low construction and maintenance costs received greater weight, followed by freedom from flies and hygiene (low potential for disease transmission). A twin pit pour-flush was judged best where water is used for anal cleaning and a double VIP was judged best where solid material is used.

Wright, 1978

Tables summarizing the characteristics of alternative systems may be helpful. However, tables over-simplify and allowance needs to be taken of variations. For example, costs for the same system may be very different, as noted in Section 8b. VIP latrines have sometimes been considered only suitable for rural areas but have operated well in some built-up places. A benefit of pit latrines of all types (simple, VIP, single pour-flush or twin pit) is that they involve no off-site facilities, but the WEDC postal survey showed that disposal of solids from full pits is a very common problem in many countries.

The following table therefore only gives the 'general' situation, which has many exceptions.

	Capital cost	Cost of operation		Usual location	Use of water	On- and off-site facilities
		Household	Communal			
Conventional sewerage	Very high	Water charges	High	Urban	Multiple connection	Sewers + sewage treatment
Non-conventional sewer (pour-flush with interceptor tank)	High	Emptying interceptor tank	High	Urban	Yard tap	Sewers + sewage treatment
Conventional septic tank and soakaway	Very high	Water + desludging	None	Low density	Multiple connection	Soakaway
Twin pit pour-flush latrine	Low/ medium	Emptying pit	None	Any	Water nearby	Soakaway
Double pit lined VIP (KVIP)	Medium	Emptying pit	None	Any	None	Soakaway
Single pit VIP	Low/ medium	None	None	Usually rural	None	Soakaway
Simple pit latrine	Low	None	None	Usually rural	None	Soakaway

Franceys, 1990

The choice of the most appropriate technology may be helped by an 'algorithm'.® A very simple algorithm is shown here.

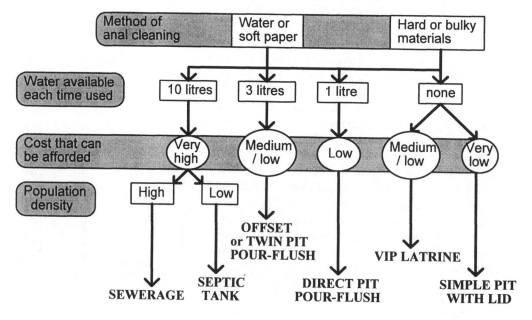

b. Information for selection

A thorough study of the local situation is desirable to enable a proper selection of technology to be made. The table that follows lists factors that need to be considered. Often much of the information is known by the intended beneficiaries or is obvious, as when sanitation is being considered by a householder in an area where there are already many other latrines.

However, when a project or programme sets out to encourage latrine construction where there are no other latrines it may be worth while carrying out a comprehensive investigation covering many of the points listed below.

Sources of information may be one or more of the following:

Community enquiry: ask for information from a cross-section of the community, making sure that minority groups are included

General enquiry: ask for information from people living or working near the place where latrines are to be constructed

Household enquiry: ask householders for information; where sanitation is encouraged for a whole community a sample of households should be interviewed; a questionnaire may be appropriate

Measurement: use a tape measure or surveyor's level, or judge distances by pacing

Observation: look around the house or plot or area

Specific enquiry: obtain information from specified source (for example, the Health Department)

Tests: Chemical or microbiological tests or analysis; occasionally testing of soil samples.

Information for selection of sanitation options

Information required	Use of information	Sources of information
Natural features		
Surface gradients	a. Surface water drainage b. Ease of access by vehicles c. Suitability for gravity sewers	Observation; measurement if the gradient is flat
Nature of soil	a. Ease of digging b. Stability of unlined pit c. Permeability	Enquiry; observation of nearby excavations; digging trial holes; percolation tests
Groundwater level	a. Likelihood of pollution b. Ease of digging c. Suitability for soakage	Enquiry; observation of nearby excavation; digging trial holes
Groundwater condition	a. Evidence of faecal pollution b. Taste and smell	Microbiological tests Enquiry; taste and smell
Surface water drainage	Liability to seasonal or perennial flooding	Observation; local enquiry about situation after heavy rainfall
The built environment		
Plot size	Is space available for latrine?	Observation; measurement of plot and building if plot small
House construction	Type of appropriate shelter	Observation
Vehicular access to plot	Can pit/tank be emptier by tanker lorry?	Observation
Water supply	Is supply suitable and sufficient for pour-flush or watercarried sanitation?	Observation; community enquiry specific enquiry to water supply organization for piped supply
Sullage disposal	Desirability/suitability of combined excreta/sullage disposal	Observation; community enquiry
The potential beneficiaries		
Family size	Size of pit, septic tank etc	Household/community enquiry
Sanitation aspirations	Preference of sanitation type	Household/community enquiry
Willingness to pay	Willingness to cover cost or part cost of sanitation improvement	Household/community enquiry
Economic level	Ability to cover cost of sanitation improvement	Government etc statistics; household/community enquiry
Prevalent diseases	Need for sanitation improvement; relevance of hygiene education	Enquiry to local clinic etc; household/community enquiry
Understanding of faecal-oral disease connection	Need for hygiene education	Enquiry to local clinic etc; household/community enquiry

Information for selection of sanitation options (continued)		
Information required	*Use of information*	*Sources of information*
Existing sanitation		
Present sanitation or method/s of defecation	Need for sanitation improvement; relevance of health education	Household/community enquiry; observation
Satisfaction with present sanitation	Felt need for improvement	Household/community enquiry
Preferred defecation posture: sit or squat	For selection of appropriate type of sanitation	Observation; household/community enquiry
Material used for anal cleaning	For selection of appropriate type of sanitation	Observation; household/community enquiry
Knowledge of sanitation options	Appreciation of options; need for sanitation extension education	Household/community enquiry
Nearby sanitation alternatives	To enable potential beneficiaries to see and examine alternatives	Enquiry to relevant sanitation or local government (LG) authority
Preferred sanitation option/s	What do beneficiaries want?	Household/community enquiry
Understanding of inputs needed to obtain preferred option/s	To enable a reasoned selection to be made following any needed guidance	Household/community enquiry
Construction		
Local availability of construction skills	Can local people carry out the required work for improvements?	Community enquiry or enquiry to sanitation or LG authority
Local availability and cost of materials	To estimate costs and the need to bring in materials	Community enquiry and enquiry to sanitation or LG authority and material suppliers
Local experience of sanitation construction	To estimate need for skill enhancement	Community enquiry and enquiry to sanitation or LG authority
Involved agencies		
Implementing sanitation agency (if any)	Whether an agency is likely to support sanitation improvement	Enquiry to agency or relevant sanitation or LG authority
Form of support by implementing agency	Possible support such as subsidy or provision of materials	Enquiry to agency
Other agencies dealing with sanitation	Possible support by technical advice etc.	Enquiry to relevant sanitation or LG authority and local NGOs
Local community organization and leadership patterns	Possible support for a sanitation improvement programme and its extension	Community enquiry

c. Evaluation

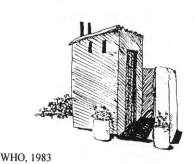

WHO, 1983

When a latrine has been built or a sanitation project has been completed it is sensible to look at it to see whether it is good. This is a form of *evaluation*. A large project may also be evaluated as it goes along, looking at each stage as it is completed.

The World Health Organization has suggested a Minimum Evaluation Procedure (MEP) that gives a relatively inexpensive and simple method of evaluating water and sanitation projects.® Three steps are given, as shown in this diagram.

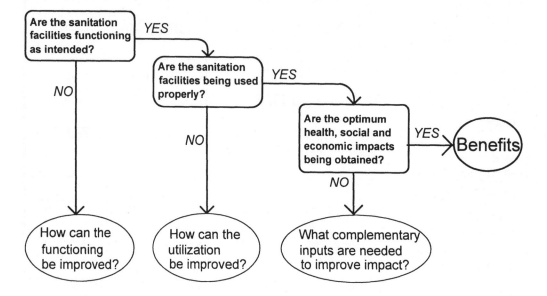

In addition to evaluating latrines or other sanitation facilities, their environmental impact should be assessed. Whenever possible, pollution should be monitored over a long period. Groundwater pollution from pits or drainfields is particularly important where drinking water is taken from nearby wells or boreholes.

d. Upgrading

Even where people have no latrine, it may be possible to upgrade their sanitation practice. For example, if the usual location is in or near water, a hygiene education programme can encourage people to chose a place where streams are not polluted. Adopting the ridge and furrow method of open defecation (Section 3a) can reduce the amount of hookworm infection.

Steps suggested for incremental improvement of sanitation in Bangladesh® were:

Hussain, 1985

1. people defecate indiscriminately (the starting point);
2. encourage the construction of simple pit latrines with a bamboo floor, so that people get accustomed to defecating at a fixed place, using whatever shelter they themselves want for privacy;
3. line pits, fit a concrete slab with a water seal and get people to think about a more permanent shelter;
4. enourage offset pits;
5. ecourage twin pits (by digging and lining a second pit).

Existing (traditional) latrines, even though they may be unsatisfactory in many ways, reflect local sociological and cultural preferences and represent an investment by the people who built them. It may be possible to upgrade them and make them hygienic and safe.® Step-by-step improvements usually have a better chance of success than do measures that require dramatic changes in the way people behave.® Making improvements rather than introducing new ideas follows the advice to 'start with what the people are doing and help them to do it better'.

Wegelin-Schuringa, 1991

Yacoob et al, 1992

Upgrading can be cost-effective. For example in Botswana the cost of a concrete slab, vent pipe, flyproof screen for vent and squatting pan was only one-seventh of the cost of building a new BOTVIP — the type of latrine being promoted. Upgrading is particularly suitable where owners like their old latrines, or where there is insufficient space for new ones.

Upgrading pit latrines

Upgrading a latrine with a single pit is only justified if space left in the pit is likely to last at least another three years. If the sides of an unlined pit show signs of erosion it is probably best to dig a new pit.

In Africa the most common type of 'unimproved' latrine has a slab made of sticks or logs topped with mud to make a fairly even floor. The timber supporting the floor

Brandberg, 1988

Causer, 1993

The end

may be in good condition if rot-proof and termite-resistant wood has been used. However, it is often virtually impossible to keep the floor clean, so hookworm transmission may be a big problem.

A mud floor can be improved so that its surface is smooth and impervious and has a slope towards the hole. Then it can be washed properly. If cement is reasonably cheap and easily obtained, the floor can be plastered with cement mortar. However, many good floors are made without cement by using local techniques. In Zimbabwe I saw cow dung left to soak in a basin of water overnight. Next day it was mixed with clay and gave a really smooth hard floor. In Zaire and Ghana soil is mixed with cassava flour, although in Ghana this is only used when there has been an exceptionally good cassava harvest. In Uganda mud is mixed with ash for termite protection and two coats of water-glass (silicate of soda) is applied to give a hard surface. In Nepal and Tanzania, thin stone slabs are sometimes put on top of mud floors.

Concrete 'SanPlat' slabs (see Section 4c) are used for upgrading timber-and-mud slabs. In the first six months of the latrine upgrading programme in Malawi, over one thousand latrines were improved in this way.® In a sanitation programme in Uganda in the early 1990s people were offered a choice of three types of latrine improvement. Lowest in cost at 45 pence was a cooking oil tin of cement (4.5kg), enough to plaster a mud floor. A Sanplat cost £1.75 and for £5 a householder could get a one metre square reinforced concrete slab with a keyhole shaped drop hole.®

One of the advantages often claimed for pour-flush pit latrines is their suitability for upgrading. If the water supply improves the pan can be flushed by a cistern and discharge to a septic tank. Alternatively the pit can be used as a settlement tank with the effluent going to a conventional or non-conventional sewerage system.

Step-by-step upgrading of existing facilities accompanied by hygiene education has proved to be the most effective means of improving environmental sanitation, but avoidance of potential pollution of water resources must always be considered.

Annex I: Selected national statistics

	GNP	inflat-ion	population		average population growth		mortality rate		population with safe water		sanitation coverage	
			total	urban	total	urban	infant	< 5 years	urban	rural	urban	rural
	US$ per person	% per year	millions	% of total popul'n	%	%	per thousand live births		%	%	%	%
	a	b	c	d	e	f	g	h	i	j	k	l
Bangladesh	220	9.1	114.4	18	2.3	6.3	91	133	39	89	40	4
Bhutan	180	8.7	1.5	6	2.1	5.3	129	205	60	30	80	3
Botswana	2790	12.6	1.4	27	3.4	8.2	35	85	100	88	100	85
Cameroon	820	3.5	12.2	42	2.9°	5.4	61	126	46	45	100	1
Egypt	600	13.2	54.7	44	2.4	2.5	57	85	95	86	80	26
Ethiopia	120	2.8	54.8	13	3.1	4.2	122	212	70	11	97	7
The Gambia	370	17.8	0.99	23°	3.1°	5.3°	135°	234	100	48	100	27
Ghana	450	38.7	15.8	35	3.2	4.3	81	137	63	41	63	60
India	310	8.5	883.6	26	2.1	3.1	79	126	86	69	44	3
Indonesia	670	8.4	184.3	32	1.8	4.6	66	86	35	33	79	30
Kenya	310	9.3	25.7	25	3.6	7.3	66	75	61°	21°	89	19
Lesotho	590	13.2	1.9	21	2.7	6.5	46	137	59	45	22	14
Malawi	210	15.1	9.1	12	3.2	6.9	134	228	97°	50°	100	81
Mozambique	60	38.0	16.5	30	2.6	8.8	162	292	44	17	53	12
Myanmar	220°	14.8	43.7	25	2.1	2.5	85°	117	79	72	50	13
Nepal	170	9.2	19.9	12	2.6	7.9	99	147	66	34	34	3
Nigeria	320	19.4	101.9	37	3.0	5.9	84	188	50	22	63	11
Pakistan	420	7.1	119.3	33	3.1	4.6	95	134	82	42	53	12
Philippines	770	14.1	64.3	44	2.4	3.8	40	46	93	72	79	63
Sierra Leone	160	60.8	4.4	34	2.4	5.1	143	253	80	20	55	31
Sri Lanka	540	11.0	17.4	22	1.4	1.5	18	21	80	55	68	45
Sudan	420°	42.8	26.5	23	2.7	4.3	99	173	55	43	89	66
Swaziland	1090	11.8	0.86	33°	3.7°	7.2°	76°	113	30		32	
Tanzania	110	25.3	25.9	22	3.0	6.8	92	178	75	46	93	58
Uganda	170	107°	17.5	12	2.6	5.4	122	190	60	30	32	60
Zambia	420°	48.4	8.3	42	3.2	4.0	107	200	76	43	76	34
Zimbabwe	570	14.4	10.4	30	3.3	5.8	47	88	95	80	95	22

a. 1992 **B**	e. 1980-92 **B**	i 1990 **W**	° for dates, or	**Sources**
b. 1980-92 **B**	f. 1980-91 **U**	j 1990 **W**	obtained from	**B** World Bank, 1994
c. 1992 **B**	g. 1992 **B**	k 1990 **W**	sources, other than	**U** UNICEF, 1993
d. 1992 **B**	h 1991 **U**	l 1990 **W**	those given here.	**W** WHO/CWS, 1992

Annex II: Glossary

aerobic: living or taking place in the presence of air or free oxygen

agency: government, donor agency, NGO or other body taking primary responsibility for a project

anaerobic: living or taking place in the absence of air or free oxygen

aqua-privy: latrine in which excreta falls directly through a submerged pipe into a watertight settling chamber below the floor and from which effluent overflows to a soakpit or drain

biochemical oxygen demand: *see* BOD

biogas: mixture of gases, mostly methane and carbon dioxide, produced in anaerobic decomposition of waste materials

BOD: biochemical oxygen demand: a measure of the amount of organic matter in wastewater

cesspit: an underground tank to retain sewage until it is removed by vacuum tanker or other means

chemical toilet: receptacle for temporary retention of excreta containing a disinfectant to retard decomposition and reduce smell

compost: humus produced by decomposition of organic matter used as fertilizer or soil-conditioner

conventional treatment: wastewater treatment processes usually employed in industrial countries

corbelling: laying bricks or blocks so that one course overhangs the course below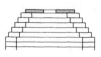

decomposition: breakdown of organic matter by the action of microorganisms

desludge: remove sludge from septic tanks etc.

drain: pipe or channel for carrying wastewater, effluent, rainwater or surface water

drainfield: area of land used for infiltration of wastewater or effluent

effluent: outgoing liquid

evapotranspiration: loss of water through plant leaves

excreta: faeces and urine

groundwater: water beneath the ground surface

helminth: a worm, particularly parasitic worms such as roundworms and hookworms

honeycomb construction: used with bricks or blocks for pit linings to allow maximum infiltration of liquid. No mortar is placed in some or all vertical joints between bricks or blocks.

humus: decomposed vegetable matter

infiltration: soakage of liquid into soil

katchi abadi: urban area in Pakistan, originally unauthorized and unplanned.

latrine: place or building, normally separate from a house or other building, for defecation

morbidity: sickness, illness

nightsoil: human excreta transported without flushing water

non-conventional sewerage: a system of sewers whose cost is less than that of conventional sewerage because of savings such as reduced diameter, depth or gradient.

offset pit: pit that is partly or wholly outside a latrine shelter.

overhung latrine: latrine from which excreta falls directly into pond or other body of water beneath.

pan: basin to receive excreta that is then flushed into a pipe, channel, tank or pit

parasite: organism that lives in or on another living organism, called the host, from which it obtains its food

pathogen: organism that causes disease

percolation: movement of liquid through soil

pollution: addition of harmful substances to water, air or soil

pour-flush latrine: latrine where a small quantity of water is poured in to flush excreta through a water seal into a pit

refuse: solid waste - rubbish or garbage

retention time: the period of time wastewater takes to go through a tank or treatment process

scum: layer of suspended solids floating on liquid

sedimentation: the process by which suspended solids in sewage settle to the bottom of a tank or pond

seepage: passage of liquid into soil; infiltration

septage: sludge removed from septic tanks

septic tank: watertight chamber for the retention, partial treatment and discharge of sewage

sewage: wastewater that is, will be, or has been carried in a sewer

sewer: pipe or conduit through which sewage is carried

sewerage system: system of interconnected sewers

shelter: screen or building of a latrine above the floor that provides privacy and protection for users

sludge: solids that have been separated from liquid by separation

soakaway: pit or trench for infiltration of liquid waste

soakpit: hole dug in the ground serving as a soakaway

squat hole: hole in the floor of a latrine through which excreta falls directly into a pit below

sullage: water that has been used for personal or domestic purposes such as washing, that does not contain excreta

superstructure: shelter

surface water: water from rain or snow lying on or flowing across the surface of the ground

toilet: place for defecation and urination; a latrine or room containing a WC

trap: water seal

vacuum tanker: vehicle-mounted tank into which the contents of septic tanks, cesspits, vaults or pits are lifted by vacuum pump

vault: watertight tank for storage of excreta

vent: pipe or chimney-like construction to facilitate escape of gases from a pit or tank

VIP latrine: ventilated improved pit latrine; pit latrine with a screened vent and fairly dark interior to the shelter

wastewater: used water discharged from domestic, commercial or industrial premises

water seal: water in a U-shaped pipe or a bowl connecting a pan to a pipe, channel or pit to prevent the escape of gases and insects into a toilet

water table: top level of groundwater

windrow: a pile of material undergoing composting

Y-junction: chamber in which liquid may be diverted along either of two pipes or channels

Annex III: Gazetteer: index of places

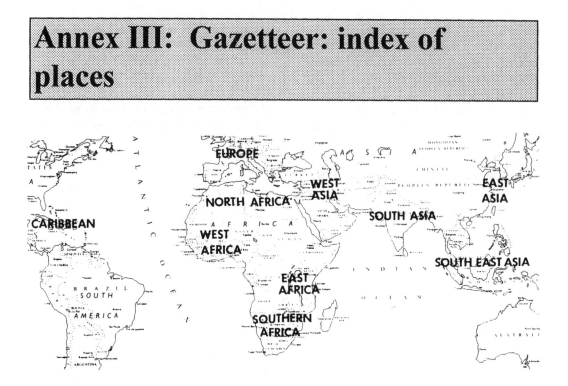

Names of countries are given in capital letters

'City' is used for a large urban area, with no particular political or demographic significance

'Region' is used for a part of a country, with no particular political or demographic significance

A

Accra - capital of GHANA: 79, 100

Addis Ababa - capital of ETHIOPIA: **108**

Africa: 2, 7, 17, 41, 73, 139

Agra - city in north INDIA: 13, 77

Ahmedabad - city in west INDIA: 31, 123

Allahabad - city in north INDIA: 13

Andhra Pradesh - state in south INDIA: **120**

ARGENTINA - South America: 68

Asia: 2, 70

AUSTRALIA - South Pacific: 81, 90

B

Baldia - *katchi abadi* in Karachi: 56, 111 113, 122

Baluchistan - PAKISTAN: 116

Bandung - city in INDONESIA: 84

Bangkok - capital of THAILAND: **4, 42**

BANGLADESH - South Asia: **4, 5, 11**, 19, 24, 26, 30, 33, 47, 51, 53, 89, 102, 104, 105, 109, 114, 115, 121, 122, 123, 131, 139

Barbados - Caribbean: **31**

BELIZE - Central America: **110**

Benares (now *Varanasi*) - city in north INDIA: **13**

Bhaktapur - town in NEPAL: **114, 133**

S - continued

Southern Africa: 54, 58, 61

SRI LANKA - South Asia: 17, 20, 23, 27, 33, 43, 51, 62, 66, 72, 102, 111

Srinagar - city in north INDIA: 26, 31

SUDAN - East Africa: 11, 25, 33, 45, 48, 76, 109

SWEDEN - Europe: 67

T

TAIWAN - East Asia: 42, 66

TANZANIA - East Africa: 3, 11, 33, 34, 43, 49, 53, 58, 60, 68, 69, 98, 107, 109, 110, 114, 140

Tegucigalpa - capital of HONDURAS: 101

Tehran - capital of IRAN: 91

Tema - city in south GHANA: 126

THAILAND - East Asia: 51, 66, 85

TOGO - West Africa: 28

Tororo - town in south UGANDA: 29

TRINIDAD AND TOBAGO - Caribbean: 115

TUNISIA - North Africa: 125

U

UGANDA - East Africa: 11, 23, 29, 39, 43, 46, 52, 109, 113, 140

UK - UNITED KINGDOM - Europe: 11, 67, 81

US(A) - UNITED STATES OF AMERICA - North America: 11, 23, 26, 38, 46, 67, 97, 98

Uttar Pradesh - state in north INDIA: 84, 126

V

VIETNAM - South Esat Asia: 66, 68, 85

W

Wanging'ombe - region of TANZANIA: 14, 60

West Africa: 73, 74, 86, 128

West Bengal - state in east INDIA: 88, 92, 104, 120. 133

West Indies: 85

Winchester - city in ENGLAND: 28

Y

Yangon (formerly *Rangoon*) - capital of MYANMAR: 3

YEMEN - West Asia: 5, 24, 33, 45

Yucatan - region in MEXICO: 33

Z

ZAIRE - central Africa: 140

ZAMBIA - Southern Africa: 6, 11, 38, 80, 86, 113

Zanzibar - island, part of TANZANIA: 15

ZIMBABWE - Southern Africa: 31, 41, 47, 48, 52, 103, 110, 115, 117, 118, 122, 133, 140

Annex IV: REFERENCES

A

AASEN, Barnt and MACRAE, Alexander, 1992. The Tegucigalpa model: water and sanitation through community management. *Waterfront*, Issue 1, February, 6.

ABEL. A H and DOHRMAN, S V, 1993. Makata pumpable VIP latrine block. *Water, sanitation, environment and development.* Proceedings of the 19th WEDC Conference, Accra, September 1993. WEDC, Loughborough. Pages 127 - 130.

ABHAYAGOONAWARDHANA, P, 1981. *WEDC coursework.*

ABU-HIJLEH, Lana, 1993. Treated wastewater reuse in the Gaza strip. *Water, sanitation, environment and development.* Proceedings of the 19th WEDC Conference, Accra, September 1993. WEDC, Loughborough. Pages 119 - 122.

ADHYA, A K and SAHA, S K, 1986. Filling characteristics of latrine pits. In *Water and sanitation at mid-Decade.* Proceedings of the 12th WEDC Conference, Calcutta, 6-9 January 1986. WEDC, Loughborough. Pages 120 - 125.

AGARWAL, A, 1981. *Water, sanitation, health - for all.* Earthscan, International Institute for Environment and Development, London.

AGARWAL, Anil and ANAND, Anita, 1982. Ask the women who do the work. *New Scientist*, vol, 96, 1330, November, 302 - 304.

AIN, Quratul, 1981. People's participation in slum upgrading. *Water, people and waste in developing countries.* Proceedings of the 7th WEDC Conference, Loughborough, September 1971. WEDC, Loughborough. Pages 10 - 14.

ALAERTS, G J, VEENSTRA, S,

BENTVELSEN, M, van DUIJL, L A and others (Alaerts *et al*), 1991. *Feasibility of anaerobic sewage treatment in sanitation strategies in developing countries.* IHE Report Series 20. International Institute for Hydraulic and Environmental Engineering, Delft.

AL-ESHAWI, Nasser, 1992. *Water supply and sanitation in rural areas of Yemen.* Paper presented at the Regional workshop on appropriate technologies for water supply and sanitation in rural areas, Amman, 4 - 8 October 1992. WHO Centre for Environmental Health Activities, Amman.

ALVARINHO, Manuel, 1991. *Personal communication.* (Head of Department of Water Supply and Sanitation, National Directorate for Water Affairs, Maputo, Mozambique).

AMOANING-YANKSON, S A, 1983. Waste Management in urban slums. In *Sanitation and water for development in Africa.* Proceedings of the 9th WEDC Conference, Harare, Zimbabe, April 1983. WEDC, Loughborough. Pages 50 - 53.

AMOS, Jim, 1993 Planning and managing urban services. In *Managing fast growing cities* (Ed. Devas and Rakodi). Longman Scientific and Technical, Harlow. Pages 132 - 152.

AMUZU, Anthony T, 1993. Sanitary aspects of groundwater supplies in Ghana. *Water, sanitation, environment and development.* Proceedings of the 19th WEDC Conference, Accra, September 1993. WEDC, Loughborough. Pages 291 - 292.

ANANKUM, Steve, 1991. *WEDC coursework.*

ANNAN, A, 1985. *The socioeconomic determinants of*

malnutration among pre-school children in Ghana. Doctoral dissertation, Cornell University, Ithaca, New York.

ANNAN, A, CROMPTON, D W T, WALTERS, D E and ARNOLD, S E, 1986. An investigation of the prevalence of intestinal parasites in pre-school children in Ghana. *Parasitology*, vol. 92, 209 - 217.

ANNAN, C E and WRIGHT, A M, 1976. *Urban waste disposal in Ghana.* Paper presented to Regional Expert Committee on Waste Disposal, Brazzaville, 25 - 29 October.

ANSTEE, Margaret Joan, 1990. Social development in Africa. In *Towards economic recovery in sub-Sahara Africa* (Ed Pickett and Singer). Pages 194 - 214.

ARLOSOROFF, Saul, TSCHANNERI, Gerhard, GREY, David, JOURNEY, William, KARP, Andrew, LANGENEGGER, Otto and ROCHE, 1987. *Community water supply: the handpump option.* The World Bank, Washington DC.

ARTHUR, J P, 1983. *Notes on the design and operation of waste stabilization ponds in warm climates of developing countries.* Technical paper No 7. The World Bank, Washington DC.

ASSAR, M, 1971. *Guide to sanitation in natural disasters.* World Health Organization, Geneva.

AZIZ, K M A, HOQUE, B A, HUTTLY, S R A, MINNATULLAH, K M, HASAN, Z, PATWARY, M K, RAHAMAN, M M and CAIRNCROSS, S, 1990. *Water supply, sanitation and hygiene education: report of a health impact study in Mirzapur, Bangladesh.* Water and Sanitation Report Series 1. The World Bank,

Washington DC.

B

BAKHTEARI, Quratul Ain and
WEGELIN-SCHURINGA,
Madeleen, 1992. *From sanitation
to development, the case of the
Baldia soakpit pilot project.*
Technical Paper Series 31. IRC,
The Hague.

BAKRI, Osman Mohamed, 1992.
*Appropriate technologies for water
supply and sanitation in rural
areas in Yemen.* Paper presented at
the Regional workshop on
appropriate technologies for water
supply and sanitation in rural areas,
Amman, 4 - 8 October 1992. WHO
Centre for Environmental Health
Activities, Amman.

BALLHATCHET, Kenneth and
HARRISON, John (Ed), 1980. *The
city in South Asia: pre-modern and
modern.* Curzon Press, London.

BANGLADESH RURAL WATER
SUPPLY AND
ENVIRONMENTAL
SANITATION PROGRAMME
(Bangladesh RWSESP), 1983. *User
perceptions and observed use of
latrines in Rahamaterpara.*
Evaluation of Latrine Technology,
Volume II. DPHE-UNICEF-WHO,
Dhaka.

BARROW, Nita, 1981. Knowledge
belongs to everyone: the challenge
in adult education and primary
health care. *Convergence*, vol.14,
2, 45 - 52.

BASKARAN, T R, 1962. *A decade
of research in environmental
sanitation (1951 - 60).* Special
Report No 40. Indian Council of
Medical Research, New Delhi.

BASKARAN, T R, 1980. Risk of
pollution of water supplies from pit
latrines. *Report of the International
Seminar on low-cost techniques for
disposal of human wastes in urban
communities.*Calcutta, February.
Annexure VI.

BAUMANN, Erick, 1993. Private
sector involvement. *Water,*

*sanitation, environment and
development.* Proceedings of the
19th WEDC Conference, Accra,
September 1993. WEDC,
Loughborough. Pages 203 - 206.

BAWA, E M, 1987. *WEDC
coursework.*

BBC, 1994. *Now wash your hands.*
Radio 4, 30 January 1994.
Produced by BBC North.

BEGAMUHUNDA, George, 1991.
WEDC coursework.

BELKHADIR, E, 1990. Rural
sanitation in Morocco. In
*Development, the environment and
health.* Proceedings of Conference,
Amman, 10 - 14 December 1988.
WHO-EMRO, Alexandria. Pages
247 - 254.

BELLARD, Brian, 1981. Financing
of low-cost sanitation schemes in
the urban areas of Botswana. In
Sanitation in developing countries.
Proceedings of a workshop on
training held in Lobatse, Botswana,
14-20 August 1980. IDRC, Ottawa.
Pages 131 - 134.

BESTOBELL ENGINEERING (SA)
Ltd, 1944. *ROEC sanitation.* Patent
No 991/1944. Bpk, South Africa.

BHATIA, H L and SASTRY, C A,
1982. Rearing of fish fry of Indian
major carps in sewage stabilization
ponds. *Water and waste
engineering in Asia.* Proceedings of
the 8th WEDC Conference,
Madras, February 1982. WEDC,
Loughborough. Pages 79 - 82.

BIELLIK, Robin J and
HENDERSON, Peggy L, 1984. The
performance of aquaprivies in Thai
refugee camps. *Waterlines*, vol. 3,
1, July, 22 - 24.

BLACKETT, Isabel, 1988.
Coordinating a national sanitation
programme: the Lesotho way.
Waterlines, vol.6, 3, January, 12 -
13.

BLAKELY, I A, MWANGAMILA,
M G, NGWAEJE, C D and SWAI,
C L, 1985. UNICEF assisted
Wanging'ombe projects. In *Water
and sanitation in Africa.*
Proceedings of the 11th WEDC

Conference, Dar es Salaam, April
1985. WEDC, Loughborough.
Pages 37 - 40.

BOMUKAMA, Sottie, 1983. *WEDC
coursework.*

BOOT, Marieke T and
CAIRNCROSS, Sandy *Ed*, 1993.
*Actions speak: the study of hygiene
behaviour in water and sanitation
projects.* IRC International Water
and Sanitation Centre, Delft, and
London School of Hygiene and
Tropical Medicine, London.

BOYDELL, R A, 1983.
Improvements to the ventilated
improved pit latrine in Tanzania.
Waterlines, vol.1, 4, April, 15 - 16.

BOYDELL, R A, 1990. *The
development of the rural water
supply and sanitation sector in
Zimbabwe between 1974 and 1987:
the design and impact of donor
supported projects.* PhD thesis.
Loughborough University of
Technology, Loughborough.

BRADLEY, R M, 1983. The choice
between septic tanks and sewers in
tropical developing countries. *The
Public Health Engineer*, vol. 11, 1,
January, 20 - 28.

BRADLEY, R M and RAUCHER, R
L, 1988. A technical and economic
comparison of nightsoil and
sewerage systems in urban areas.
Water S A, vol. 14, 1, January, 49 -
57.

BRANDBERG, Bjorn, 1983. *The
latrine project, Mozambique.*
IDRC-MR58e. International
Development Research Centre,
Ottawa.

BRANDBERG, Bjorn, 1985. Why
should a latrine look like a house?
Waterlines, vol. 3, 3, January, 24 -
26.

BRANDBERG, Bjorn, 1988. Low-
cost sanitation in Malawi - the
urban to rural approach. In
Developing World Water, vol.
3. Grosvenor Press International,
London. Pages 28 - 30.

BRANDBERG, Bjorn, 1991a. The
SanPlat system: lowest cost
environmental sanitation. In

Infrastructure, environment, water and people. Proceedings of the 17th WEDC Conference, Nairobi, 19 - 23 August. WEDC, Loughborough. Pages 193 - 196.

BRANDBERG, Bjorn, 1991b. *Planning, construction and operation of public and institutional latrines.* Hesawa Programme Management, Stockholm.

BRANDBERG, Bjorn, 1993. A sanitation revolution in Bangladesh? *Waterlines*, vol. 11, 4, April, 25 - 27.

BRANDT, Willie, 1980. *North-South: a programme for survival.* The report of the independent commission on international development issues. Pan Books, London

BRISCOE, J and FERRANTI, D de, 1988. *Water for rural communities - helping people help themselves.* The World Bank, Washington DC.

BRITISH STANDARDS INSTITUTION (BSI), 1983. *British Standard Code of Practice for design and installation of small sewage treatment works and cesspools: BS 6279: 1983.* BSI, London.

BUREN, Ariane van, 1979 (Ed). *A Chinese biogas manual.* Translated from the Chinese by Michael Crook. IT Publications, London.

BUREN, Ariane van, McMICHAEL, Joan, CACERES, Roberto and CACERES, Armando, 1984. Composting latrines in Guatemala. *Ambio*, vol.13 , 4, 274 - 277.

BURGERS, Lizette, BOOT, Marieke and WIJK-SIJBESMA, Christine van, 1988. *Hygiene education in water supply and sanitation programmes: literature review with selected and annotated bibliography.* Technical Paper No 27. IRC, The Hague.

BURGESS, Rob, 1993. Rural school sanitation pilot project. *Water, sanitation, environment and development.* Proceedings of the 19th WEDC Conference, Accra,

September 1993. WEDC, Loughborough. Pages 131 - 133.

C

CAIRNCROSS, Sandy, 1988. *Small scale sanitation.* Ross Bulletin No 8. The Ross Institute, London.

CAIRNCROSS, Sandy, 1989. Water supply and sanitation: an agenda for research. *Journal of Tropical Medicine and Hygiene*, vol. 92, 301 - 314.

CAIRNCROSS, Sandy, 1992. *Sanitation and water supply: practical lessons from the Decade.* Water and sanitation discussion paper No 9. The World Bank, Washington DC.

CALDWELL, Elfreda Larson, 1938. Pollution flow from a pit latrine where permeable soils of considerable depth exist below the pit. *Journal of Infectious diseases*, vol. 62, 3, 225 - 258.

CARLTON-SMITH, C H and COKER, E G, 1985. Manurial value of septic-tank sludge on grassland. *Grass and forage science*, vol. 40, 411 - 417.

CARROLL, R F, 1985. Mechanised emptying of pit latrines in Africa. In *Water and sanitation in Africa.* Proceedings of the 11th WEDC Conference, Dar es Salaam, 15 - 19 April 1985. WEDC, Loughborough. Pages 29 - 32.

CARROLL, R F and ASHALL, G J, 1989. A permeable lining for seepage pits. *Waterlines*, vol. 8, 1, July, 30 - 32.

CASSERLY, M J P, 1978. *Personal communication.*

CAUSER, Helen, 1993. Low-cost techniques for improving latrines in a demonstration village in Uganda. *Waterlines*, vol. 11, 3, January, 5 - 7. Also *personal communication.*

CHADHA, Skylark and STRAUSS, Martin, 1991. *Promotion of rural sanitation in Bangladesh with private sector participation.* Swiss Development Corporation, Dhaka, Bangladesh.

CHAMBERS, Robert, 1983. *Rural development: putting the last first.* Longman, London.

CHARNOCK, Gary, 1983. Patel promotes people participation. *World Water*, vol. 6, 12, December, 31 - 32.

CHAUDHURI, Nirad C, 1965. *The continent of Circe.* Chatto and Windus, London.

CHAUHAN, Sumi Krishna *et al*, 1983. *Who puts water in the taps?* Earthscan, London.

CLARKE, Lorna E, 1984. *Knowledge, attitudes and practices related to water and sanitation: result of a study in six villages of North-West Frontier Province of Pakistan.* UNICEF, Islamabad.

COFFEY, Manus, 1988. Low cost latrine emptying vehicle. In *Water and urban services in Asia and the Pacific.* Proceedings of the 14th WEDC Conference, Kuala Lumpur, 11 - 15 April 1988. WEDC, Loughborough. Pages 77 - 80.

COGHLAN, Alan, 1993. Compost toilet brings relief to beauty spots. *New Scientist*, vol. 138, part 1868, 10 April, page 18.

COLIN, Jeremy, 1992. *Personal communication.*

CONSORTIUM ON RURAL TECHNOLOGY, 1981. *Rural sanitation: technology options.* Institute of Social Studies Trust, New Delhi.

COWAN, J P and JOHNSON, P R, 1985. Reuse of effluent to agriculture in the Middle East. In *Reuse of sewage effluent.* Thomas Telford, London.

CROMPTON, D W T, 1991. The challenge of parasitic worms. *Transactions of the Nebraska Academy of Sciences*, vol. 18, 73 - 86.

CROSS, Piers, 1985. Existing practices and beliefs in the use of human excreta. *IRCWD News*, No 23, December, 2 - 4.

CSO: CENTRAL STATISTICAL ORGANIZATION, MYANMAR, (C S O) 1989. *Evaluation survey of*

latrine construction project.
Ministry of Planning and Finance,
Yangon.

CURTIS, C F and HAWKINS, P M,
1982, Entomological studies of on-
site sanitation systems in Botswana
and Tanzania. *Transactions of the
Royal Society of Tropical Medicine
and Hygiene*, vol. 76, 1, February,
99 - 108.

D

DANIDA: Danish International
Development Agency (Danida),
1991. *Village sanitation: survey of
629 households carried out in
Matale District during April 1991.*
Report No A21. Support to the
rural water supply and sanitation
sector in Matale, Polonnaruwa and
Anuradhapura Districts for the
National Water Supply and
Drainage Board, Sri Lanka.
Kampsax-Kruger, Copenhagen.

DANIEL. R R and LLOYD. B J,
1980. Microbiological studies on
two Oxfam sanitation units
operating in Bengali refugee
camps. *Water Research*, vol. 14,
11, 1567 - 1571.

DAVIDSON, Phil, 1993. Cholera
menace returns to Mexico. *The
Independent*, 31 August.

DAVIS, Jan, GARVEY, Gerry and
WOOD, Michael, 1993.
*Developing and managing
community water suppliesl. Oxfam,
Oxford.*

DE KRUIJFF, G J, 1986. Sanitation
improvements in Indonesian
kampongs. In *Water and sanitation
at mid-Decade*. Proceedings of the
12th WEDC Conference, Calcutta,
6-9 January 1986. WEDC,
Loughborough. Pages 176 - 179.

DE KRUIJFF, G J, 1987. A feasible
sanitation alternative. In
Developing World Water, vol. 2.
Grosvenor Press International,
London. Pages 52 - 53.

DENNIS-ANTWI, Jemima A, 1993.
Participatory methods in hygiene
communication. *Water, sanitation,*

environment and development.
Proceedings of the 19th WEDC
Conference, Accra, September
1993. WEDC, Loughborough.
Pages 278 - 281.

DE ROOY, Carl, 1989. *Personal
communication.*

DEUTERONOMY. *The Bible.*
Deuteronomy, chapter 23, verse 13.

DEVELOPING WORLD WATER,
1988. Emptying latrines - the
Lesotho experience. *Developing
World Water* (Ed. Pickford). vol. 3.
Grosvenor Press International,
London.

DEWIT, Michael and SCHENK,
Hans, 1989. *Shelter for the poor in
India: issues in low cost housing.*
Manohar Publications, New Delhi.

DOOGAR, R K, 1990. *WEDC
coursework.*

DORSCH, Margaret M, SCRAGG,
Robert K R, McMICHAEL,
Anthony J, BAGHURST, Peter A
and DYAR, Kenneth F, 1984.
Congenital malformation and
maternal drinking water supply in
rural South Australia: a case study.
American Journal of Epidemiology,
vol.
119, 4, April, 473 - 486.

DREWS, R J L C, 1983. *Pond
systems for the purification and
disposal of domestic wastewater
from small communities: use,
design, operation and maintenance.*
CSIR Guide K15. National Institute
for Water Research, Pretoria, South
Africa.

DUQUEHIN, F L, 1978. *Personal
communication.*

DWYER, D J. 1975. *People and
housing in Third World cities.*
Longman, London.

E

EDWARDS, Peter, 1992. *Reuse of
human wastes in aquaculture: a
technical review.* UNDP-World
Bank Water and Sanitation
Program. Water and Sanitation
Report 2. The World Bank,
Washington DC.

EGBUNIWE, N, 1980. Alternative
excreta disposal systems in eastern
Nigeria. *Water and waste
engineering in Africa.* Proceedings
of the 6th WEDC Conference,
Zaria, March 1980. WEDC,
Loughborough. Pages 137 - 140.

EL-KATSHA, Samiha and WATTS,
Susan, 1993. A multifaceted
approach to health education: a
case study from rural Egypt.
*International Quarterly of
Community Health Education*,
(1992-1993), vol.13, 2, 139-149.

EL-KATSHA, Samiha, YOUNIS,
Awatif, EL-SEBAIE, Olfat and
HUSSEIN, Ahmed, 1989. *Women,
water and sanitation: household
water use in two Egyptian villages.*
The American University in Cairo
Press, Cairo.

ELMENDORF, Mary and
BUCKLES, Patricia, 1980.
Sociocultural aspects of water
supply and excreta disposal.
Appropriate technology for water
supply and sanitation, vol. 5. The
World Bank, Washington DC.

ENFO NEWS, 1989. Reuse of
wastes. *Enfo News*, vol. 11, 4, 6,10.

ENFO NEWS, 1993. Fresh water and
population pressure. *ENFO News*,
vol. 14, 4, January, 1 - 3.

ENGLAND, R, DE KRUIJFF, G J
and SONI, P, 1980. *The pit latrines
of Lamu: 600 years of 'illegal '
sanitation.* Housing Research and
Development Unit, University of
Nairobi, Nairobi, Kenya.

EPA (Melbourne): ENVIRONMENT
PROTECTION AGENCY, 1979.
Comparison of sewerage and
common effluent drainage for
country townships. EPA Report No.
65/79. EPA, Melbourne, Australia.

ENVIRONMENTAL HEALTH,
1993. Water supply and sanitation
in Honduras. *Environmental
Health*, No 19, July.

ESRAY, Steven A, COLLETT, Jim,
Miliotis Marianne D,
KOORNHOF, Hendrick A and
MAKHALE, Popi, 1989. The risk
of infection from *Giardia lamblia*

due to drinking water and latrines among preschool children in rural Lesotho. *International Journal of Epidemiology*, vol. 18, 1, 248 - 253.

ESRAY, S A, FEACHEM, R G and HUGHES, J M, 1985. Interventions for the control of diarrhoeal diseases among young children: improving water supplies and excreta disposal facilities. *Bulletin of the World Health Organization*, vol. 63, 4, 757-772.

ESRAY, Steven A, POTASH, James B, ROBERTS, Leslie and SHIFF, Clive, 1990. *Health benefits from improvements in water supply and sanitation: survey and analysis of the literature on selected diseases.* WASH Technical Report No 66. WASH, Arlington, Va, USA.

ETHERTON, David, 1980. *Water and sanitation in slums and shanty towns.* UNICEF report TRH 10. UNICEF, New York.

F

FAROOQ, Shaukat and ANSARI, Zafar I, 1983. Wastewater reuse in Muslim countries: an Islamic perspective. *Environmental Management*, vol. 7, 2, 119 - 123.

FEACHEM R G, 1986. Preventing diarrhoea: what are the policy options? *Health Policy and Planning*, vol.1 , 2, 109 - 117.

FEACHEM R G, BRADLEY D, GARELICK, H and MARA, D D, 1983. *Sanitation and disease: health aspects of excreta and wastewater management.* John Wiley and Sons, Chichester.

FEACHEM, R G, GUY, M W, HARRISON, Shirley, IWUGO, K O, MARSHALL, Thomas, MBERE, Nomtuse, MULLER, Ralph and WRIGHT, A M, 1983. Excreta disposal facilities and intestinal parasitism in urban Africa: preliminary studies in Botswana, Ghana and Zambia. *Trans Royal Society of Tropical Medicine and Hygiene*, vol. 77, 4,

515 - 521.

FEACHEM, R G, MARA, D D and IWUGO, K O, 1979. *Alternative sanitation technologies for urban areas in Africa.* Public Utilities Report No. RES 22. The World Bank, Washington DC .

FELICIANO, G and FLAVIER, J, 1967. Strategy of change in the barrio: a case study of rural waste disposal. In *Communication and change in the developing countries* (Ed Lerner and Schramm). East-West Center Press, Honolula.

FERNANDO, Vijita, 1982. *Cooperating with non-governmental groups: a lavatory without walls.* Paper presented at the UNDP/NGO Water Decade Consultation Meeting.

FLANAGAN, Donna, 1988. *Human resources development in water and sanitation programmes: case studies from Togo, Sri Lanka, Philippines, Zaire and Thailand.* Training Series No 3. IRC, International Water and Sanitation Centre, The Hague.

FORMAN, David, 1987. Gastric cancer, diet and nitrate exposure, *British Medical Journal*, 28 February, 294, 528 - 529.

FRANCEYS, Richard, 1988. Low-cost sanitation in Juba. In *Developing World Water*, vol. 3. Grosvenor Press International, London. Pages 25 - 27.

FRANCEYS, Richard, 1990. Guide to sanitation selection. Technical Brief No 23. *Waterlines*, vol. 8, 3, January, 15 - 18. Also in *The worth of water; technical briefs on health, water and sanitation*. Intermediate Technology Publications, London. Pages 93 - 96.

FRANCEYS, Richard, 1991. *Community management.* Technical Brief No 30. *Waterlines* , vol. 9, 2, July, 15 - 19. Also in *The worth of water: technical briefs on health, water and sanitation.* Intermediate Technology Publications, London. Pages 121 - 124.

FRANCEYS, Richard, PICKFORD, John and REED, Robert, 1992. *A guide to the development of on-site sanitation.* World Health Organization, Geneva.

FUREDY, Christine and GHOSH, Dhrubajyoti, 1984. Resource-conserving traditions and waste disposal: the garbage farms and sewage-fed fisheries of Calcutta. *Conservation and Recycling*, vol. 7, 2-4, 159-165.

G

GARBAN, Yandi Ahmed, 1990. *WEDC coursework.*

GIBBS, Ken, 1984. Privacy and the pit privy: technology or technique. *Waterlines*, vol. 3, 1, July, 19 - 21.

GILLANDERS, George, 1940. Rural housing. *J Royal Sanitary Institute*, vol. 60, 6, 230 - 240.

GLENSVIG, Leo and GLENSVIG, Dorte, 1989. Pour-flush toilets and waste stabilization ponds in a refugee camp. *Waterlines*, vol. 8, 1, July, 2 - 4.

GOETHERT, Reinhart *et al*, 1979. Cluster layouts in high density urban situations. In *Human consequences of crowding* (Ed Gurkaynak and LeCompte). Plenum Press, New York.

GOI: GOVERNMENT OF INDIA, 1990. *People, water and sanitation: what they know, believe and do in rural India.* National Drinking Water Mission. GOI, New Delhi.

GOI/RWSG-SA: GOVERNMENT OF INDIA and REGIONAL WATER SUPPLY & SANITATION GROUP - SOUTH ASIA, 1992. *Technical guidelines on twin pit pour flush latrines.* Ministry of Urban Development, GOI, and UNDP/World Bank water & Sanitation Program, RWSG-SA, New Delhi.

GOSS, Patrick, 1992. VIP latrines: are they always the best alternative? *Waterlines*, vol. 11, 1, July, 13 - 14.

GOYDER, Catherine, 1978.

Voluntary and government sanitation programmes. In *Sanitation in developing countries* (Ed Pacey). John Wiley & Sons, Chichester. Pages 162 - 167.

GRACE, J, 1986. Department of Forestry and Natural Resources, University of Edinburgh, *Personal communication*.

GREENHALGH, S J, 1984. *Low cost sanitation in urban areas in developing countries*. PhD thesis, Leeds. Department of Civil Engineering, Leeds University.

GUPTA, Rajiv, 1983. Are community biogas plants a feasible proposition? *World Health Forum*, vol. 4, 4, 358 - 361.

H

HABICHT, J-P, DAVANZO, J and BUTZ, W P, 1988. Mother's milk and sewage: their interactive effects on infant mortality. *Pediatrics*, vol. 81, 3, 456 - 461.

HALL, David and ADAMS, Michael, 1991. *Water, sanitation, hygiene and health in the Qabane Valley, Lesotho: Report on a survey carried out by Sechaba Consultants for the water supply and sanitation programme of Tebellong Hospital Primary Health Care Department*. Sechaba Consultants, Qacha's Nek, Lesotho.

HARDOY, Jorge E, CAIRNCROSS, Sandy and SATTERTHWAITE, David, 1990. *The poor die young: housing and health in Third World cities*. Earthscan Publications, London.

HARDOY, Jorge E, MITLIN, Diana and SATTERTHWAITE, David, 1992. *Environmental problems in Third World cities*. Earthscan, London.

HARDOY, Jorge E and SATTERTHWAITE David, 1985. Third world cities: the environment of poverty. *J World Resources Institute*, 45 - 57.

HARPHAM, Trudy, LUSTY, Tim and VAUGHAN, 1988. *In the shadow of the city: community health and the urban poor*. Oxford University Press, Oxford.

HARRIS, Mollie, 1984. *Cotswold Privies*. Chatto & Windus, London.

HARRIS, Mollie, 1990. *Privies galore*. Alan Sutton, Stroud.

HARRIS, R B, MASKELL, A D, NJAU, F Z and PICKFORD, John, 1981. Dar-es-Salaam sewerage and sanitation study. In *Appropriate technology in civil engineering*. Institution of Civil Engineers, London. Pages 67 - 69.

HARRISON, J B, 1980. Allahabad: a sanitary history. In *The city in south Asia* (Ed. Ballhatchet and Harrison). Curzon Press, London.

HARRISON, Paul, 1987. *The greening of Africa: breaking through in the battle for land and food*. Grafton Books, London.

HASAN, Arif, 1992. Karachi's poor neighbourhoods achieve low-cost sanitation. *Source*, vol. 4, 2, 24 -25.

HERBERT, James R, 1985. Effects of components of sanitation on nutritional status: findings from south Indian settlements. *International Journal of Epidemiology*, vol. 14, 1, 143 - 152.

HINDHAUGH, G M A, 1973. Night-soil treatment. *The Consulting Engineer*, September, 47, 49.

HOEFNAGELS, H A M, DHARMAGUNAWARDENE, PENDLEY, C, KRABBE, O J aand SENARATNE (Hoefnagels *et al*), 1986. Integrated rural water supply and sanitation programme. In *Water and sanitation at mid-Decade*. Proceedings of the 12th WEDC Conference, Calcutta, January 1986. WEDC, Loughborough. Pages 130 - 136.

HOGG, C and DYER, E, 1958. Main sewerage and sewage purification Kuala Lumpur, Malaysia. In *Conference of Civil Engineering Problems Overseas*. Institution of Civil Engineers, London.

HOLLAND, R J, 1977. The improvement of domestic sanitation in unsewered areas of Kenya. In *Engineering for health in hot countries*. Proceedings of the 4th WEDC Conference, Loughborough, 25 - 27 September 1977. WEDC, Loughborough. Pages 59 - 81.

HOPCRAFT, Arthur, 1968. *Born to hunger*. Pan Books, London.

HOWARD, A and WAD, Y D, 1931. *The waste products of agriculture*. Oxford University Press, London.

HOWARD, J C, 1977. The Oxfam sanitation unit in Bangladesh. In *Planning for water and waste in hot countries*. Proceedings of the 3rd WEDC Conference, Loughborough, September 1976. WEDC, Loughborough. Pages 103 - 106.

HUBLEY, John, 1987. Communication and health education planning for sanitation programmes. *Waterlines*, vol. 5, 3, January, 2 - 5.

HUDA, Shamsul, 1993. Subsidy, to what extent? *Water, sanitation, environment and development*. Proceedings of the 19th WEDC Conference, Accra, September 1993. WEDC, Loughborough. Pages 174 - 176.

HUNT, Steven, 1986. Lucrative latrines. *IDRC Reports*, vol. 15, 4, October, page 13.

HUSSAIN, M A, 1985. (Formerly Chief Engineer, Department of Public Health Engineering, Dhaka, Bangladesh. *Discussion with author*.

I

IKEDA, Ichiro, 1972. Experimental study of treatment of night soil by the wet air oxidation process. *Water Research*, vol. 6, 967 - 979.

ILUSTRE, Oscar I, 1980. Metro Manila sewerage and sanitation project. Report of the International Seminar on low-cost techniques for disposal of human wastes in urban communities.Calcutta, February. Annexure VII.

INDIAN STANDARDS
INSTITUTION, 1986. *Code of
practice for installation of septic
tanks. Part 1: design criteria and
construction. IS 2470 (Part 1).*
Indian Standards Institution, New
Delhi. Sub-paragraph 3.1.3.

IRC NEWSLETTER, 1992.
Successful promotion accelerates
sanitation coverage in Bangladesh.
IRC Newsletter No 211, October.
Pages 3 - 4.

ISELEY, Raymond B, FAIIA, Scott,
ASHWORTH, John, DONOVAN,
Richard and THOMSON James,
1986. *Framework and guidelines
for Care water supply and
sanitation projects.* WASH
Technical Report No 40. WASH,
Arlington.

IWUGO, Kenneth O, MARA, D D
and FEACHEM, R G, 1978a.
Sanitation studies in Africa. A
research study of the World Bank.
Sanitation Site Report Number 1,
Ibadan, Nigeria. The World Bank,
Washington DC.

IWUGO, Kenneth O, MARA, D D
and FEACHEM, R G, 1978b.
Sanitation studies in Africa. A
research study of the World Bank.
Sanitation Site Report Number 4,
Zambia (Lusaka and Ndola). The
World Bank, Washington DC.

J

JEEYASEELEN, S, LOHANI, B N
and VIRARAGHAVAN, T
(Jeeyaseelen *et al*), 1987. *Low-cost
rural sanitation - problems and
solutions.* ENSIC, Bangkok.

JEWELL, W J, HOWLEY, J B and
PERRIN, D R, 1975. Design
guidelines for septic tank treatment
and disposal. *Progress in Water
Technology*, vol. 7, 2, 191 - 205.

JOINT COMMITTEE ON
MEDICAL ASPECTS OF WATER
QUALITY, 1984. *Advice on nitrate
in drinking water in relation to a
suggested cancer risk.* Department
of Health and Social
Security/Department of the

Environment. HMSO, London.

K

KAI, Prem, 1990. *WEDC
coursework.*

KALBERMATTEN, John M, 1991.
Water and sanitation for all, will it
become reality or remain a dream?
Water International, vol. 16, 3,
September, 121 - 126.

KALBERMATTEN, J M, JULIUS, D
S and GUNNERSON, C G
(Kalbermatten *et al*), 1982.
*Appropriate sanitation
alternatives: a technical and
economic appraisal.* World Bank
studies in water supply and
sanitation 1. John Hopkins
University Press, Baltimore.

KALIMANZILA, F B, 1980. *WEDC
coursework.*

KARP, Andrew W, 1992.
Contracting NGOs to implement
rural water and sanitationprojects in
Bolivia. *Waterlines*, vol. 11, 1,
July, 23 - 27.

KAUNDA, K, 1972. *You hold the
key to the success in participatory
democracy.* Zambian Information
Service, Lusaka.

KAWATA, Kuzuyoshi, 1978. Of
typhoid fever and telephone poles:
deceptive data on the effect of
water supply and privies on health
in tropical countries. *Progress in
Water Technology*, vol. 11, 1/2, 37
- 43.

KHAKETLA, T, RAMONAHENG,
Mamonaheng R and JACKSON,
Barry M, 1986. Schools sanitation
in Lesotho. In *Water and sanitation
at mid-Decade.* Proceedings of the
12th WEDC Conference, Calcutta,
January 1986. WEDC,
Loughborough. Pages 137 - 140.

KHAN, Akhtar Hameed, 1992.
Orangi Pilot Project Programs.
Orangi Pilot Project - Research and
Training Institute, Karachi.

KILAMA, W and MINJAS, J, 1985.
The mounting Culex p.
quinquefasciatus problem in urban
East Africa. In *Water and*

sanitation in Africa. Proceedings of
the 11th WEDC Conference, Dar es
Salaam, April 1985. WEDC,
Loughborough.

KING Rudith S and DINYE
Romanus, 1993. Women and
children in water and sanitation
development. *Water, sanitation,
environment and development.*
Proceedings of the 19th WEDC
Conference, Accra, September
1993. WEDC Loughborough.
Pages 235 - 236.

KIPLING, Rudyard, 1937. *Something
of mys* K *elf.* . Macmillan, London.

KITAWAKI, Hidetoshi *et al*, 1994.
Nightsoil and graywater
management in Japan. *INTEP
Newsletter*, No 5, June, 2 - 4.

KLEIN, I, 1973. Death in India, 1871
- 1921. *J Asian Studies*, vol. 32, 4,
639 - 659.

KLIGLER, I J, 1921. *Investigation
on soil pollution and the relation of
the various types of priviesto the
spread of intestinal infections.*
Monograph No 15. The Rockfeller
Institute for Medical Research,
New York.

KOCHAR, Vijay, 1978. Culture and
hygiene in rural West Bengal. In
Sanitation in developing countries
(Ed Pacey). Pages 176 - 184.

KOTALOVA, J, 1984. *Personal and
domestic hygiene in rural
Bangladesh.* SIDA, Stockholm.

L

LACEY, Linda and OWUSU, Steven
E, 1988. Squatter settlements in
Monrovia, Liberia: the evolution of
housing policies. In *Slum and
squatter settlements in Sub-
Saharan Africa: toward a planning
strategy* (Ed. Obudho and
Mhlanga). Praeger, New York.

LAMBTON, Lucinda, 1978. *Temples
of convenience.* Gordon Fraser,
London.

LANGSHAW, C L, 1952. Sanitation
in the West Indies. *Journal of the
Institute of Sanitary Engineers*, vol.
51, 82 - 109.

LA TROBE, B E and ROSS, W R, 1992. Full-scale operation of forced aeration composting garbage and nightsoil. In *65th Annual Conference of the Water Environment Federation*, New Orleans, September.

LAVER, Sue, 1986. Communications for low-cost sanitation in Zimbabwe. *Waterlines*, vol. 4, 4, April, 26 - 28.

LAVER, Sue, 1988. Learning to share knowledge - a Zimbabwean case study. *Waterlines*, vol. 6, 3, January, 6 - 8.

LEA, John P and COURTNEY, John M (Ed), 1985. *Cities in conflict: studies in the planning and management of Asian cities*. World Bank, Washington, DC.

LETTINGA, G, de MAN, A, van der LAST, A R M *et*, 1993. Anaerobic treatment of domestic sewage and wastewater. *Water Science and Technology*, vol. 27, 9, 67 - 73.

LEWIS, W John, FOSTER, Stephen S D and DRASAR, Bohumil, 1982. *The risk of groundwater pollution by on-site sanitation in developing countries - a literature review*. IRCWD Report No 01/82. International Reference Centre for Wastes Disposal, Duebendorf.

LOCHERY, Peter W S and ADU-ASAH, Seth T, no date. *Building and operating multi-compartment VIP latrines*. Lagos.

LOHANI, Kumar and GUHR, Ingo, 1985. *Alternative sanitation in Bhaktapur, Nepal: an exercise in community participation*. GTZ, Eschborn.

LOWDER Stella, 1986. *Inside Third World Cities*. Croom & Helm, London.

LUONG, T V, NJAU, F and KAHESA, A Y, 1993. Towards self-management, water and sanitation. *Water, sanitation, environment and development*. Proceedings of the 19th WEDC Conference, Accra, September 1993. Pages 5 - 7.

M

McAUSLAN, Patrick, 1985. *Urban land and shelter for the poor*. Earthscan, London.

McCOMMON, Carolyn, WARNER, Dennis and YOHALEM David (McCommon *et al*), 1990. *Community management of rural water supply and sanitation services*. UNDP-World Bank Water and Sanitation Program Discussion Paper Series, DP Number 4. World Bank, Washington, DC.

MACGARRY, Brian, 1983. The development of the Blair VIP latrine. *Waterlines*, vol. 1, 4, April, 13 - 14.

McGILVRAY, James, 1984. *Contact*, No 81, October. Page 1.

McMICHAEL, Joan K, 1978. The double septic bin in Vietnam. In *Sanitation in developing countries* (Ed Pacey). John Wiley & Sons, Chichester. Pages 110 - 114.

McNEIL, G M, 1978. *Personal communication*. (Military Vehicles and Engineering Establishment, Christchurch).

MAGARA, Yasumoto, 1990. *Personal communication*. (Director of Sanitary Engineering, Institute of Public Health, Ministry of Health and Welfare, Tokyo).

MAITRA, M S, 1978. Sanitation for the urban poor in Calcutta. In *Sanitation in developing countries* (Ed Pacey). Wiley, Chichester. Pages 144 - 152.

MAJUMDER, N, PRAKASAM, T B S and SURYPRAKASAM, M V, 1960. A critical study of septic tank performance in rural areas. *J Instn Engrs (India)*, vol. 40, 12, PH1, 743 - 761.

MAKHATHA, S N, 1987. Single and double pits in Lesotho. In *Rural development in Africa*. Proceedings of the 13th WEDC Conference, Lilongwe, April 1987. WEDC, Loughborough. Pages 32 - 35.

MAKWALI, Saad R, 1992. *WEDC coursework*.

MALAN, W M, 1964. *A guide to the use of septic tank systems in South Africa*. CSIR research report No 219. CSIR, Pretoria.

MALOMBE, Joyce, 1993. Sanitation and solid waste disposal in Malindi. *Water, sanitation, environment and development*. Proceedings of the 19th WEDC Conference, Accra, September 1993. WEDC, Loughborough. Pages 134 - 136.

MANCY, K H, 1993. A new perspective on rural water supply and sanitation. *Water Science and Technology*, vol.27, 9, 1 - 5.

MARA, D D, 1976. *Sewage treatment in hot climates*. John Wiley & Sons, London.

MARA, D D, 1994. Ventilated improved pit latrines. *Oasis*, Spring/Summer, page 13.

MARA, D D and CAIRNCROSS, Sandy, 1989. *Guidelines for the safe use of wastewater and excreta in agriculture and aquaculture: mesures for public health protection*. World Health Organization, Geneva.

MARA, D D and SINNATAMBY, G S, 1986. Rational design of septic tanks in warm climates. *Public Health Engineer*, vol.14, 4, 49 - 55.

MARAIS, G v R, 1973. Sanitation and low cost housing. In *Water quality: management and pollution control problems* (Ed. Jenkins). Pergamon, Oxford. Pages 115 - 125.

MARAMAH, Enias, 1990. *WEDC coursework*.

MATHEBULA, Mpho, 1987. Sanitation, hygiene and children. In *Developing World Water*, Volume 2. Grosvenor Press International, London. Pages 38 - 39.

MEADOWS, Brian S, 1983. Fish production in waste stabilization ponds. In *Sanitation and water for development in Africa*. Proceedings of the 9th WEDC Conference, Harare, April 1983. WEDC, Loughborough. Pages 39 - 43.

MERTENS, Thierry E, JAFFAR, Shabbar, FERNANDO, Malcolm A, COUSENS, Simon N and

FEACHEM, R G, 1992. Excreta disposal behaviour and latrine ownership in relation to the risk of childhood diarrhoea in Sri Lanka. *International Journal of Epidemiology*, vol. **21**, 6, 1157 - 1164.

MEYER, Kathleen, 1989. *How to shit in the woods: an environmentally sound approach to a lost art*. Ten Speed Press, Berkeley.

MIELDAZIS, J J. 1934. Organic manure from street refuse and night-soil at Mysore City, India. *The Indian Medical Gazette*, February, 87 - 93.

MISRA, D K, 1988. Cultural attitudes in rural sanitation. *Health for the millions* (Delhi), vol. 14, 4, August, 2 - 5.

MOES, W and ZWAGG, R R, 1984. Low cost solutions often beat sewers. *World Water*, September, 56 - 57.

MOHAMMED, Kazi Noor, 1990. *WEDC coursework.*

MOHANRAO, G J, 1973. Waste water and refuse treatment and disposal in India. In *Environmental health engineering in hot climates and developing countries* (Ed Pickford). WEDC, Loughborough. Pages 69 - 86.

MOORE, Helen A, De LA CRUZ, Enrique and VARGAS-MENDEZ, Oscar, 1965. Diarrheal disease studies in Costa Rica: IV. The influence of sanitation upon the prevalence of intestinal infection and diarrheal disease. *American Journal of Epidemiology*, vol. 82, 2, 162 - 184

MORGAN, Peter, 1977. The pit latrine - revived. *Central African J Medicine*, vol. 23, 1 - 4.

MORGAN, Peter, 1988. Village-level sanitation programmes in Zimbabwe. *Waterlines*, vol. 6, 3, January, 9 - 11.

MORGAN, Peter, 1990. *Rural water supplies and sanitation: a text from Zimbabwe's Blair Resarch Laboratory*. Macmillan, Basingstoke.

MORGEN, Peter, 1994. Simpler, cheaper VIP latrines. *Dialogue on Diarrhoea*, issue no 57, June-August, page 4.

MORGAN, Peter and CHIMBUNDE, Ephraim, 1982. Improved ventilated pit latrines for rural areas, *Appropriate technology*, vol. 9, 2, September, 10, 12 - 14.

MORGAN, Peter and CLARKE V de V, 1978. Specialized developments of pit latrines. In *Sanitation in developing countries* (Ed Pacey). John Wiley & Sons, Chichester. Pages 100 - 104.

MORGAN, Peter and MARA, D D, 1982. *Ventilated improved pit latrines: recent developments in Zimbabwe*. World Bank Technical Paper No 3. The World Bank, Washington DC.

MORRIS, Duncan, 1993. Thinking things through. *Water, sanitation, environment and development*. Proceedings of the 19th WEDC Conference, Accra, September 1993. WEDC, Loughborough. Pages 8 - 11.

MORROW, Richard H, 1983. A primary health care strategy for Ghana. In *Practising health for all* (Ed Morley, Rohde and Williams). Oxford University Press, Oxford. Pages 272 - 299.

MOSER, Caroline O N, 1991. Women and self-help housing projects: a conceptual framework for analysis and policy-making. In *Beyond self-help housing* (Ed Mathéy). Mansell Publishing, London. Pages 53 - 73.

MOSER, Caroline O N and PEAKE, Linda, 1987. *Women, human settlements, and housing*. Tavistock Publications, London.

MOWFORTH, K and AGGARWAL, K K, 1985. Development of the Buguruni-type VIP. In *Water and sanitation in Africa*. Proceedings of the 11th WEDC Conference, Dar es Salaam, 15 - 19 April 1985. WEDC, Loughborough.

MOYO, Isaac, 1992. *WEDC coursework*

MPOWE K, B, 1992. *WEDC coursework*

MUGENYI, George, 1993. *WEDC coursework.*

MULLER, Maria S, 1988. The improvement of Chawama, a squatter settlement in Lusaka, Zambia. In *Slum and squatter settlements in Sub-Saharan Africa: towards a planning strategy*. Praeger, New York.

MULLER, Maria, KIRANGO, Jasper and RYNSBURGER, Jaap (Muller *et al*),1993. An alternative pit latrine emptying system. *Water, sanitation, environment and development*. Proceedings of the 19th WEDC Conference, Accra, September 1993. WEDC, Loughborough. Pages 137 - 139.

MULLICK, M A, 1987. *Socio-economic aspects of rural water supply and sanitation: a case study of the Yemen Arab Republic*. The Book Guild, Lewes.

MUNIR, Amir, 1991. *WEDC coursework*.

MUNYAKHO, D, 1992. Poverty and health go hand-in-hand. *World Health*, November-december, 6 - 7.

MUNYAKHO, Dorothy, 1994. *Personal communication*.

MUWONCE, John, 1993. *WEDC coursework*.

MWAYANGUBA, Charles, 1991. *WEDC coursework*.

MYINT, Thein Maung and AYE, U Ba, 1988. *Evaluation of the health impact of tube well water supply in dry zone rural communities in Burma*. Unpublished document. Department of Medical Research, Ministry of Health, Rangoon.

N

NAIPAUL, V S, 1981. *Among the believers*. Penguin Books, Harmondsworth.

NARAYAN-PARKER, Deepa, 1985. Developing toilet designs for the Maldives. *Waterlines*, vol. 4, 2, October, 26 - 30.

NENE, Moses Nhlamhla, 1991. *WEDC coursework.*

NEPAL H M Government, undated. *Drinking water supply and sanitation sector review and development plan (1991-2000)..* Kathmandu.

NEPAL, MINISTRY OF PANCHAYAT AND LOCAL DEVELOPMENT (Nepal, Panchayat), undated. *design, construction and use of pit latrines.* Ministry of Panchayat and Local Development, Kathmandu

NEW VISION, 1993. News item and photograph. *New Vision, Uganda,* August 1993.

NGO Forum, 1993. *Annual Report 1992.* NGO Forum for Drinking Water Supply and Sanitation, Dhaka.

NICHOLS, Paul, 1982. *Juba urban area sanitation survey: report of findings: sanitation facilities.* Unpublished report, Juba.

NIEDRUM, Susanne, 1993. The need for hygiene education. *Water, sanitation, environment and development.* Proceedings of the 19th WEDC Conference, Accra, September 1993. WEDC, Loughborough. Pages 15 - 17.

NIELSON, John Hebo and CLAUSON-KAAS, Jes, 1980. *Appropriate sanitation for urban areas.* Cowiconsult, Virum.

NIMPUNO, Krisno, 1978. Scandinavian mouldering latrines and the biopot. In *Sanitation in developing countries* (Ed Pacey). John Wiley & Sons, Chichester. Pages 115 - 119.

NIMPUNO, Krisno, 1981. Vietnam's sanitation system. *Water, people and waste in developing countries.* Proceedings of the 7th WEDC Conference, Loughborough, September 1981. WEDC, Loughborough. Pages 43 - 48.

NOSTRAND, John van and WILSON, James G, 1983. *The ventilated improved double-pit latrine: a construction manual for Botswana.* TAG Technical Note No

3. The World Bank, Washington DC.

NWOKOCHA, A I C, 1990. *WEDC coursework.*

NYASALAND, various dates. *Annual reports of the Nyasaland Medical Department.*

O

OAKLEY, H R, 1983. Urban sanitation and surface water drainage. In *Water supply and sanitation in developing countries* (Ed B J Dangerfield). Water Practice Manual, 3. Institution of Water Engineers and Scientists, London.

OBENG, Letitia E, 1991. *The right to health in tropical agriculture.* International Institute of Tropical Agriculure, Ibadan.

OLUWANDE, P A, 1978. The potential of the aqua-privy: Nigerian experience. In *Sanitation in developing countries* (Ed Pacey). John Wiley & Sons, Chichester. Pages 88 - 91.

OLUYEMI, I O, 1972. *Refuse and sewage disposal.* Conference, Nigerian Society of Engineers, Benin City, 6 - 8 December.

OO, Saw and THWIN, Khin Maung, 1987. *An evaluation study of household latrines in Burma.* UNICEF, Rangoon.

OTIS, R, 1983. *Small diameter gravity sewers: an alternative wastewater collection method for unsewered communities.* Report prepared for the United States Environmental Protection Agency (USEPA). Municipal Environmental Research Laboratory, Office of Research and Development, USEPA, Cincinnati.

OTIS, R J and MARA, D D, 1985. *The design of small bore sewer systems.* TAG Technical Note No 14. The World Bank, Washington DC.

OWUSU, S E, 1982. *Behavioural aspects of rural sanitation in*

Ghana. National Workshop on Rural Sanitation in Ghana. Accra, 28 September - 1 October.

P

PAQUI, Hilda, 1988. Low-cost sanitation in Mozambique. *Waterlines,* 7, 1, July, 6 - 7.

PARAMASIVAN, S, 1993. *WEDC coursework.*

PASHA, Hafiz A and McGARRY, Michael G (*Editors*), 1989. *Rural water supply and sanitation in Pakistan.* World Bank Technical Paper Number 105. The World Bank, Washington, DC.

PASTEUR, D, 1979. The Ibadan comfort stations programme: a case-study of the community development approach to environmental health improvement. *Journal of Administration Overseas,* vol. 18, 1, 46 - 58.

PATHAK, Bindeshwar, 1985. *Personal communication.* (Founder and Chairman, Sulabh International).

PAUDYAL, I P, 1992. *WEDC coursework*

PAZLAR, Karel, 1994. *Sierra Leone water and sanitation baseline data study.* UNICEF, Freetown.

PEEL, C, 1967. The problem of excremental disease in tropical Africa. *Journal of Tropical Medicine and Hygiene,* vol. 70, June, 141 - 152.

PEEL, C, 1976. The public health and economic aspects of composting night soil with municipal refuse in tropical Africa. In *Planning for water and waste in hot countries.* Proceedings of the 3rd WEDC Conference, September 1976. WEDC, Loughborough. Pages 25 - 36

PICKFORD, John, 1980. *The design of septic tanks and aqua-privies.* BRE Overseas Building Notes. No 187, September. Overseas Division, Building Research Establishment, Gartree.

PICKFORD, John, 1988. Sewerage.

Technical Brief No 10. *Waterlines*, vol. 6, 4, April, 15 - 18. Also in *The worth of water: technical briefs on health, water and sanitation*. Intermediate Technology Publications, London, 1991. Pages 65 - 68.

PICKFORD, John, 1991. Public and communal latrines. Technical Brief No 28. *Waterlines* , vol. 9, 3, 15 - 19. Also in *The worth of water: technical briefs on health, water and sanitation*. Intermediate Technology Publications, London. Pages 113 - 116.

PICKFORD, John, 1992. Latrine vent pipes. Technical Brief No 31. *Waterlines*, vol. 10, 3, January, 15 - 18. Also in *The worth of water: technical briefs on health, water and sanitation*. Intermediate Technology Publications, London, 1991. Pages 125 - 128.

PICKFORD, John, 1993. Low cost sanitation and other GARNET topics. In *Water, sanitation, environment and development*. Proceedings of the 19th WEDC Conference, Accra, September 1993. WEDC, Loughborough. Pages 313 - 316.

PICKFORD, John, 1994. Affordable sanitation for low income communities. In *Affordable water supply and sanitation*. Proceedings of the 20th WEDC Conference, Colombo, August 1994. WEDC, Loughborough. Pages 3 - 6.

PICKFORD, John and FRANCEYS, Richard, 1989. *Arriyadh rising groundwater management study: domestic water conservation*. Report for the Arriyadh Development Authority. WEDC, Loughborough.

PINIDIYA, H, no date. *Human waste disposal systems for low income settlements in Sri Lanka*.

POLPRASERT, C, WANGSUPHACHART, S and MUTTAMARA, S, 1980. Composting nightsoil and water hyacinth in the tropics. *Compost Science/Land Utilization*, vol. 21,

2, 25 - 27.

PONTIUS, F W, 1993. Nitrates and cancer: is there a link? *J American Water Works Association*, vol. 85, 4, 12 and 14.

PRADT, L A, 1971. Some recent developments in night soil treatment. *Water Research*, vol. 5, 507 - 521.

PUDNEY, John, 1954. *The smallest room*. Michael Joseph, London.

R

RAHMAN, Mizanur, RAHAMAN, M Mujibur, WOJTYNIAK, Bogdan and AZIZ, K M S, 1985. Impact of environmental sanitation and crowding on infant mortality in rural Bangladesh. *The Lancet*, 6 July, ii, 28 - 31.

RAILTON, Frank A, 1978. *Personal communication*. (Now Porthcawl, Wales; East Africa, 1930 - 1953).

RAJ, Mulkh, 1991. *Financing of urban infrastructure in India*. HUDCO, New Delhi.

RAMAN, V and CHAKLADER, N, 1972. Upflow filters for septic tank effluents. *Journal of the Water Pollution Control Federation*, vol. 44, 8, August, 1552 - 1560.

RAO, J R N, 1976. *The new pour-flush privy: construction method and installation procedure*. Ministry of Health, Suva.

RAWLINSON, R, 1871. Discussion: The treatment of town sewage by A Jacob. *Minutes of Proceedings of the Institution of Civil Engineers*, vol. 32, 371-420.

READ, Geoffrey H, 1980. Aspects of low cost sanitation in Africa. *Report of the International Seminar on low-cost techniques for disposal of human wastes in urban communities*. Calcutta, February. Annexure IXfc.

REED, R A, 1994. Low cost sanitation in China. *Science, Technology and Development*, vol. 11, 3, December, 245-259.

REED, R A and VINES, Marcus, 1989. Reduced cost sewerage -

does it work? In *Water, engineering and development in Africa*. Proceedings of the 15th WEDC Conference, Kano, Nigeria, 3 - 7 April. WEDC, Loughborough. Pages 111 - 114.

REMEDIOS, A P, 1981. Ecological balance in Goa. In *Appropriate technology in civil engineering*. Institution of Civil Engineers, London. Pages 46 - 48.

REYBURN, Wallace, 1989. *Flushed with pride : the story of Thomas Crapper*. Pavilion Books, London.

REYNOLDS, Reginald, 1943. *Cleanliness and godliness*. George Allen & Unwin, London.

RIBEIRO, Edgar F, 1985. *Improved sanitation and environmental health conditions: an evaluation of Sulabh International's low cost sanitation project in Bihar*. Sulabh International, Patna.

RIJNSBURGER, Jaap, 1991. Emptying pit latrines: WASTE fills a vacuum in Dar es Salaam, Tanzania. *AT Source*, vol. 18, 2, 29 - 33.

ROBERTS, Martin, 1987. Sewage collection and disposal. In *Affordable housing projects: a training manual: Readings*. Prepared for the United Nations Centre for Human Settlements (Habitat). Development Planning Unit, London.

ROBSON Emma, 1991. China's centuries-old recyling tradition gears for the future. *Source*, vol. 3, 4, December, 5 - 11.

ROSENHALL, L, 1990. Water supply and sanitation in rural Burma - towards convergence. *Water Quality Bulletin*, vol. 15, 1, January, 46 - 51, 64, 65.

ROY, A K, 1990. *Review of low cost sanitation technologies in India*. Assignment report, 15 October - 29 December 1989.

ROY, A K, CHATTERJEE, P K, GUPTA, K N, KHARE, S T, RAU, B B and SINGH, R S, 1984. *Manual on the design, construction and maintenance of low-cost pour-*

flush waterseal latrines in India.
TAG Technical Note Number 10.
The World Bank, Washington DC.
RYAN, Beverley A and MARA, D
D, 1983. *Ventilated improved pit
latrines: vent pipe design
guidelines.* TAG Technical Note
No 6. The World Bank,
Washington DC.

S

SAGAR, Gyan, 1983. A dwarf septic
tank developed in India.
Waterlines, vol. 2, 1, July, 22 - 23.
SAGAR, Gyan and CHOURASIA, H
S, 1990. Design of biogas plant
based on human excreta. Paper
presented at the *International
Conference on Water and Waste
Water* Barcelona, 24 - 27 April.
SAHC: SOUTH AUSTRALIAN
HEALTH COMMISSION (SAHC),
1986. *Common effluent drainage
schemes.* Health Surveying
Services, SAHC, Adelaide.
SALE, Charles, 1930. *The specialist.*
Putman, London.
SAMANTA, B B, 1993. *Low-cost
options in rural water supply and
sanitation: approaches and
strategies in India.* WEDC project
report. WEDC Loughborough.
SARMA, Sanjib and JANSEN, Marc,
1989. *Use and maintenance of low
cost sanitation facilities study of
Srinagar city, Jammu and Kashmir.*
Human Settlement Management
Institute, New Delhi.
SCHERTENLEIB, Roland and
HAWKINS, Peter, 1983. *Problems
related to emptying on-site excreta
disposal systems.* Paper presented
at the International Seminar on
Human Waste Management for
Low Income Settlements, Bangkok,
16 - 22 January 1983.
SELL, Jack, 1981 (formerly
UNICEF, Sudan). *Personal
communication.*
SHAFIUDDIN and BACHMAN,
Sally, no date. *Vietnamese latrines
at Gonoshasthaya Kendra.*
Unpublished report. Gonoshasthaya

Kendra, Savar, Dhaka.
SHALALAM, Abul Basher M, 1986.
Septage collection system
economics. In *Water and sanitation
at mid-Decade.* Proceedings of the
12th WEDC Conference, Calcutta,
January 1986. WEDC,
Loughborough. Pages 104 - 107.
SHAW, V A, 1962. *A system for the
treatment of nightsoil and
conserving tank effluent in
stabilization ponds.* CSIR Reprint
No 166. Pretoria.
SHUVAL, H I, ADIN, Avner,
FATTAL, Badri, RAWITZ,
Eliyahu and YEKUTIEL, 1986.
*Wastewater irrigation in
developing countries: health effects
and technical solutions.* World
Bank Technical Paper Number 51.
The World Bank, Washington DC.
SHUVAL, H I, YEKUTIEL P and
FATTAL B, 1984. Epidemiological
evidence for helminth and cholera
transmission by vegetables irrigated
with wastewater: Jerusalem - a case
study. *Water Science and
Technology*, vol. 17, 433 - 442.
SIERRA LEONE: Ministry of
Health, 1989. *Primary health care
baseline survey: Western Area.* The
Planning, Management,
Information and Statistics Unit,
Ministry of Health, Freetown.
SILVA, Kalinga Tudor and
ATHUKORALA, Karunatissa,
1991. *The watta-dwellers: a
sociological study of selected urban
low-income communities in Sri
Lanka.* University Press of
America, Lanham.
SIMPSON-HEBERT, Mayling, 1993.
Sanitation: the unmet challenge.
Environmental Health, No 20,
October, 1- 4.
SINHA, Bakshi D and GHOSH, Arun
K, 1990. *Evaluation of low-cost
sanitation: liberation, training and
rehabilitation of scavengers.*
Arnold Publishers, New Delhi.
SINNATAMBY, G, 1990. Low cost
sanitation. In *The poor die young*
(Ed Hardoy et al). Earthscan
Publications, London. Pages 127 -

157.
SINNATAMBY, G, MARA, D D
and McGARRY, M, 1986. Shallow
systems offer hope to slums. *World
Water*, vol. 9, No 1, 39-41.
SKINNER, Brian, 1994. *Personal
communication.*
SMITH, Michael D, 1994. *Personal
communication.*
SOTO, Harnando de, 1989. *The other
path: the invisible revolution in the
Third World.* Tauris, London.
SRIDHAR, M K C and
OMISHAKIN, M A, 1985. An
evaluation of the water supply and
sanitation problems in Nigeria.
*Journal of the Royal Society of
Health*, vol. 105, 2, 68 - 72.
SSOZI, Disan, 1991. *WEDC
coursework.*
STOBERT, J C, 1935. *The glory that
was Greece.* Revised by F N Pryce.
Appleton Century Co, New York.
STONER, Carol Hupping, 1977.
Goodbye to the flush toilet. Rodale
Press, Emmaus, Pa.
STRACHEY, Lytton, 1979. *Eminent
Vistorians.* Chatto and Windus,
London.
STRAUSS, Martin, 1983.
Community water supply and
sanitation programme of the
Western Development Region of
Nepal. *IRCWD News*, 18/19,
December, 1 - 10.
STRAUSS, Martin, 1985. Health
aspects of nightsoil and sludge use
in agriculture and aquaculture: Part
II: Survival of excreted pathogens
in excreta and faecal sludges.
IRCWD News, No 23, 4 - 9.
STRAUSS, Martin, 1993. Treatment
of sludges from on-site sanitation.
*Water, sanitation, environment and
development.* Proceedings of the
19th WEDC Conference, Accra,
September 1993. WEDC,
Loughborough. Pages 143 - 148.
STRAUSS, Martin and
BLUMENTHAL, Ursula J, 1990.
*Use of human wastes in agriculture
and aquaculture: utilization
practices and health perspectives.*
IRCWD Report No 08/90.

International Reference Centre for Waste Disposal, Duebendorf.

STRUYK, Raymond, 1989. *Assessing housing needs and policy alternatives in developing countries*. Urban Institute Report 88-4. University Press of America.

SUBRAMANIUM, S K, 1978. Biogas systems and sanitation. In *Sanitation in developing countries*. (Ed Pacey). John Wiley & Sons, Chichester. Pages 191 - 194.

SUNDARARAMAN, Veena, 1986. *Social feasibility study in the role of women in rural development*. SNDT University, Bombay.

SWAFFIELD, J A and WAKELIN, R H M, 1988. Low water use sanitation - the design and site evaluation of a three litre flush volume WC. In *Developing World Water*, Volume 3. Grosvenor Press International. Pages 351 - 353.

SYARIKAT GIBSON PERNIAGAAN, no date. *Gibson plastic water-seal latrine pan*. Manufacturer's leaflet. Kuala Lumpur.

T

TANNAHILL, J, 1966. Aspects of sewage disposal in Rhodesia. *Journal and Proceedings of the Institute of Sewage Purification*, No 5, 459 - 463.

TANZANIA, UNITED REPUBLIC OF, PRIME MINISTER'S OFFICE AND IRC (Tanzania), 1984. *Water, sanitation and village health: a community organization and participation approach in Tanzania*. Paper presented at the interregional seminar on women and the International Drinking Water Supply and Sanitation Decade, Cairo, Egypt, 12 - 16 March 1984. INSTRAW, Santo Domingo.

THACKER, Sankarshan, 1993. Brahmins twist sacred thread round ear when urinating. *The Statesman*, Calcutta, 19 November, page 4.

THE URBAN EDGE, 1982. World

Bank urban operations - II. *The Urban Edge*, **6**, 9, 1 - 5.

THEUNYCK, Serge and DIA, Mamadou, 1981. The young (and the less young) in infra-urbain areas in Mauritania. *African Environment*, vol. 4, 205 - 233.

THOMAS, P R and RAMAMURTHY, K N, 1984. Environmental improvement in slums through community participation. *Water and sanitation in Asia and the Pacific*. Proceedings of the 10th WEDC Conference, Singapore, August 1984. WEDC, Loughborough. Pages 83 - 86.

TOBIN, V, 1985. Sanitation training in Nepal. *Waterlines*, **4**, 2, October, 13 - 15.

TUKULA, Felix, 1992. *WEDC coursework*

TURNER, J A, 1894. *Twang Tung or five years in South China*. Partridge & Co, London. (Reprinted 1986 by OUP, Hong Kong)

TURNER, J A, 1914. *Sanitation in India*. The Times of India, Bombay.

U

UGBE, Utiang P, 1990. *WEDC coursework*.

UNCHS: UNITED NATIONS CENTRE FOR HUMAN SETTLEMENTS, 1980. *Physical improvement of slums and squatter settlements*. Report of an Ad Hoc Expert Group Meeting held in Nassau, 31 January - 4 February 1977. CHS/R/80-1/S. UNCHS, Nairobi.

UNCHS: UNITED NATIONS CENTRE FOR HUMAN SETTLEMENTS, 1982. *Appropriate infrastructure services, standards and technology*. Report of the *ad hoc* expert working group meeting on appropriate services, standards and technologies for upgrading slums and squatter areas and rural settlements. Nairobi, 2 - 9 November 1981. HS/OP/82-10. UNCHS, Nairobi.

UNCHS: UNITED NATIONS CENTRE FOR HUMAN SETTLEMENTS, 1984. *A review of technologies for the provision of basic infrastructure in low-income settlements*. HS/40/84/E. UNCHS, Nairobi.

UNCHS: UNITED NATIONS CENTRE FOR HUMAN SETTLEMENTS, 1986a. *Sociocultural perspective of sanitation in Nepal: a survey report*. UNCHS, Nairobi.

UNCHS: UNITED NATIONS CENTRE FOR HUMAN SETTLEMENTS, 1986b. *Community participation in low-cost sanitation - training module*. UNCHS, Nairobi.

UNCHS: UNITED NATIONS CENTRE FOR HUMAN SETTLEMENTS, 1989. *The maintenance of infrastructure and its financing and cost recovery*. UNCHS, Nairobi.

UNDP-WORLD BANK WATER AND SANITATION PROGRAM and PROWESS (UNDP-World Bank), 1990. *Rural sanitation in Lesotho: from pilot project to national program*. The World Bank, Washington DC.

UNESCAP: UNITED NATIONS ECONOMIC AND SOCIAL COMMISSION FOR ASIA AND THE PACIFIC, 1984, *Improvement of slums and squatter settlements - infrastructure and services*. UNESCAP, Bangkok, Thailand.

UNICEF, 1992. *The state of the world's children 1992*. OUP, Oxford.

UNICEF, 1993. *The state of the world's children 1993*. OUP, Oxford.

UNICEF/DPHE: UNICEF and DEPARTMENT OF PUBLIC HEALTH ENGINEERING, 1980. *Enduse evaluation of water seal latrines: nine village profile of Kaliakoir in Bangladesh*. UNICEF and DPHE, Dacca (Dhaka).

UNITED NATIONS, 1956. *20th Report of the Administrative*

Committee on Coordination to the United Nations Economic and Social Council. Annex III. Document E/2931. United Nations, New York.

UNIVERSITY OF ZIMBABWE DEPARTMENT OF LAND MANAGEMENT (University of Zimbabwe), 1982. *Environmental Study of the Sabi Valley, Manicaland.* University of Zimbabwe, Harare.

UNRAU, G O, 1978. Water seal pit latrines. In *Sanitation in developing countries* (Ed Pacey). John Wiley & Sons, Chichester. Pages 104 - 106.

US AGENCY FOR INTERNATIONAL DEVELOPMENT (USAID), 1973. *Problems of voluntary agencies in African develpment.* USAID, Washington DC.

USEPA: UNITED STATES ENVIRONMENTAL PROTECTION AGENCY, 1984. *Handbook: Septage treatment and disposal.* EPA-625/6-84-009. USEPA, Cincinnati.

USEPA: UNITED STATES ENVIRONMENTAL PROTECTION AGENCY, 1991. *Manual: Alternative wastewater collection systems.* EPA/625/1-91/024. USEPA, Cincinnati.

V

VINCENT, L J, ALGIE, W E and MARAIS, G van R (Vincent *et al*), 1961. *A system of sanitation for low cost high density housing.* African Housing Board, Lusaka.

VINES, Marcus and REED, R A, 1990. Low-cost unconventional sewerage. *Waterlines*, vol. 9, 1, July, 26 - 29.

W

WAGNER, E G and LANOIX, J N, 1958. *Excreta disposal for rural areas and small communities.*

World Health Organization, Geneva.

WAKELIN, R, SWAFFIELD, J and BOCORRO, R., 1987. Low volume flush WC design. In *Rural water and engineering development in Africa.* Proceedings of the 13th WEDC Conference, Lilongwe, August 1987. WEDC, Loughborough.

WAN, Philip, 1992. Social mmobilization for sanitation. In *Water, environment and management.* Proceedings of the 18th WEDC Conference, Kathmandu, September 1992. WEDC, Loughborough. Pages 28 - 31.

WARNER, D B and LAUGERI, L, 1991. Health for all: the legacy of the water decade. *Water International*, vol. 16, 3, September, 135 - 141.

WATT, Jim and LAING, Richard O, 1985. Teaching aids for water and sanitation. *Waterlines*, **3**, 4, April, 25 - 27.

WEDC: WATER ENGINEERING AND DEVELOPMENT CENTRE (WEDC), 1988. Discussion Group Report: Sewerage", in *Water and urban services in Asia and the Pacific.* Proceedings of the 14th WEC Conference, Kuala Lumpur, September. WEDC, Loughborough

WEGELIN-SCHURINGA, Madeleen, 1991. *On-site sanitation: building on local practice.* IRC, The Hague.

WEIR, John M, WASIF, Ibrahim Messack, HASSAN, Farag Rizk, ATTIA, Salah el Din Moh and KADER, Mohamed Abdel, 1952. An evaluation of health and sanitation in Egyptian villages. *J Egyptian Public Health Association*, vol. 27, 55 - 122.

WHEELER, D and CARROLL, R F, 1989. The minimisation of microbiological hazards associated with latrine wastes. *Water Science and Technology*, vol. 21, 3, 35 - 42.

WHITTINGTON, Dale, LAURIA, Donald T, WRIGHT, Albert M,

CHOE, Kyeongae, HUGHES, Jeffrey A and SWARNA, Venkateswarlu, 1992. *Household demand for improved sanitation services: a case study of Kumasi, Ghana.* Water and sanitation report 3, UNDP-World Bank Water and Sanitation Program. The World Bank, Washington DC.

WHO: WORLD HEALTH ORGANIZATION, 1951. *Expert committee on school health .services. Technical Report Series No 30. WHO, Geneva.

WHO: WORLD HEALTH ORGANIZATION, 1982. *Benefits to health of safe and adequate drinking water and sanitary disposal of human waste: imperative considerations for the International Drinking Water Supply and Sanitation Decade.* EHE/82.32. WHO, Geneva.

WHO: WORLD HEALTH ORGANIZATION, 1983. *Minimum evaluation procedure (MEP) for water supply and sanitation projects.* WHO, Geneva, Switzerland.

WHO: WORLD HEALTH ORGANIZATION, 1987. *Evaluation of the strategy for health for all by the year 2000: Seventh report on the world health situation.* Volume 1, Global review. WHO, Geneva.

WHO: WORLD HEALTH ORGANIZATION, 1991. Surface water drainage for low-income communities. WHO, Geneva.

WHO: WORLD HEALTH ORGANIZATION, 1992. *Our planet, our health.* Report of the World Commission on health and environment. WHO, Geneva.

WHO: WORLD HEALTH ORGANIZATION, 1993a. *Guidelines for cholera control.* WHO, Geneva.

WHO: WORLD HEALTH ORGANIZATION, 1993b. *Guidelines for drinking-water quality.* 2nd edition. Volume 1: recommendations. WHO, Geneva.

WHO/CWS: WORLD HEALTH ORGANIZATION, CWS UNIT, 1992. *The International Drinking Water Supply and Sanitation Decade: end of decade review (as at December 1990).* WHO/CWS/92.12. WHO, Geneva.

WHO/EMRO: WORLD HEALTH ORGANIZATION, REGIONAL OFFICE FOR THE EASTERN MEDITERRANEAN, 1992. *Drinking water supply and sanitation sector support project in Egypt: rural sanitation technology.* WHO/EMRO, Alexandria.

WHO/SEARO: WORLD HEALTH ORGANIZATION, SOUTH-EAST ASIA REGION, 1988. *Acceleration of national programmes on sanitary disposal of human excreta: Report of an inter-country workshop, New Delhi, 27 - 31 October 1986.* SEARO, New Delhi.

WHO/SEARO: WORLD HEALTH ORGANIZATION, SOUTH-EAST ASIA REGION, 1993. *New directions for hygiene and sanitation promotion: the findings of a Regional Informal Consultation, New Delhi, 19-21 May 1993.* WHO/CWS/93.8. WHO, Geneva.

WIGGLESWORTH, Professor Sir Vincent B, 1978. *Personal communication.*

WILCOCK, S C, 1965. *Medical advance, public health and social evolution.* Pergamon, London.

WILLIAMS, Chris, 1987. Choices in pit latrine emptying. In *Rural water and engineering development in Africa.* Proceedings of the 13th WEDC Conference, Lilongwe. WEDC, Loughborough. Pages 28 - 31.

WILLIAMS, David F, no date. *A report on family latrine trials at Tongi and Demra resettlement camps in Bangladesh.* Unpublished report.

WILLIAMSON, J R, 1983. Towards community managed drinking water schemes in Nepal. *Waterlines,* vol. 2, 2, October, 8 -

13.

WILSON, H E, 1978. *Personal communication.* (Institute of Geological Sciences, London).

WILSON, James G, 1983. The implementation of urban and rural sanitation programmes in Botswana. In *Sanitation and water for development in Africa.* Proceedings of the 9th WEDC Conference, Harare, Zimbabwe, April 1983. WEDC, Loughborough. Pages 46 - 49.

WINBLAD, Uno, 1994. Urban alternatives: the dry-box. *Dialogue on Diarrhoea,* issue no 57, June-August, page 6.

WINBLAD, Uno, KILAMA, Wen and TORSTENSSON, K, 1985. *Sanitation without water.* Macmillan, Basingstoke.

WORLD BANK, 1992. *World development report, 1992: development and the environment.* Oxford University Press, New York.

WORLD BANK, 1994. *World development report, 1994: infrastructure for development.* Oxford University Press, New York.

WORLD HEALTH, 1988. The declaration of Alma-Ata. *World Health,* August/September, 16 - 17.

WORLD WATER, 1983. What is a pour-flush waterseal latrine? *World Water,* vol. 6, 12, December, p34.

WRIGHT, A M, 1978. A review of rural excreta disposal systems. *Progress in Water Technology,* vol. 11, 1/2, 211 - 218.

WRIGHT, A M, 1982. *Report on mission to United Republic of Tanzania.* UNDP, New York.

WRIGHT, A M, OWUSU, S E and HANDA, V K, 1978. Availability of latrines in a developing country. In *Sanitation in developing countries* (Ed. Pacey). Wiley, Chichester. Pages 4 - 10.

WRIGHT, Lawrence, 1960. *Clean and decent: the fasciniating history of the bathroom and the water closet.* Routledge & Kegan Paul,

London.

Y

YACOOB, May, BRADDY, Barri and EDWARDS, Lynda, 1992. *Rethinking sanitation: adding behavioral change to the project mix.* WASH Technical Report No 72. WASH, Arlington.

YACOOB, May and ROARK, Philip, 1990. *Tech Pak: steps for implementing rural water supply and sanitation projects.* WASH Technical Report No 62. WASH, Arlington

Z

ZACHER, W, 1982. The significance of water and sanitation for primary health care workers in developing countries. *Internat J Hygiene Education,* vol. 2, 1, 21 -30.

Annex V: INDEX